Success to Stalemate in South Korea

John Benton

authorHOUSE®

AuthorHouse™
1663 Liberty Drive
Bloomington, IN 47403
www.authorhouse.com
Phone: 1-800-839-8640

© 2010 John Benton. All rights reserved.

No part of this book may be reproduced, stored in a retrieval system, or transmitted by any means without the written permission of the author.

First published by AuthorHouse 9/9/2010

ISBN: 978-1-4520-1725-9 (hc)
ISBN: 978-1-4520-1726-6 (sc)
ISBN: 978-1-4520-1724-2 (e)

Library of Congress Control Number: 2010906157

Printed in the United States of America

INTRODUCTION

This book is a sequel to a previous book I wrote, published in 2003, entitled "Should Be Soldiers," which was about the author's experiences as the medical officer in an infantry battalion medical aid station during the first part of the Korean War. Often described as "America's Forgotten War," it started on 25th June 1950, only five years after the end of World War II, when the communist North Korean Peoples' Army suddenly and massively invaded the democratic South Korea. The earlier book covered the period from the start of the war to the end of 1950, which includes the frantic defense of the Naktong Perimeter, the reconquest of South Korea, the ill-fated and poorly planned invasion of North Korea, and the subsequent disastrous retreat of the American Army forces after the Chinese suddenly came into the war in late November, 1950.

Events in this book are described as how I saw and understood them at the time they happened from my viewpoint as the medical officer now in a regimental medical collecting station. Potential legacy problems again mandated a semi-fictional approach in order to tell the real story.

This book picks up the story from the previous one, again as seen from the viewpoint of the author, as noted above then a medical officer in an infantry battalion medical collecting station. It begins just after General Ridgway had taken over command from the elderly and very unpopular General MacArthur in December 1950. The American army, so beaten down by their calamitous forced withdrawal from North Korea, was to be literally turned around into a major fighting force by General Ridgway. It become the larger part and leader of what was now called the United Nation forces, as many other countries began sending troops to help hold back the threat of communism spreading in southeast Asia. The communist Chinese and the North Koreans were soon pushed back up to and a bit beyond the 38th Parallel, the prewar line between the two Koreas, by the spring of 1951.

Peace talks then commenced, although they dragged on for two more years. The battle lines became stabilized, even static, as the talks glacially proceeded. When the author was rotated back to the US in early September, where this story ends, the battle lines hadn't changed significantly since the previous May. However, the armies soon went into bunker warfare, like the Siege of Vicksburg in the Civil War and the trench warfare in France in World War I. There were still to be very bloody battles, if on a smaller scale, mostly over the possession of higher ground, while indecisive discussions continued. It was to be two more years, while the battle lines changed little, before the war was stopped with an inconclusive armistice.

The writer made copious notes about these events, even to the point of recording conversations, and sent them home by mail. Again, the semi-fictional approach had to be used, just as with the first book. Dates, locations and activities are described as we knew them to be at the time. The descriptions of military units and locations are sometimes, but not always, based on composites of several, just as are the descriptions of the officers and men involved. Nonetheless, all the events described actually occurred and are described as accurately as we could understand them at the time they happened, although later studies may have rewritten the stories about some of them.

CHAPTER 1

The building could have once been some sort of a barn. It had one large and two smaller rooms. Since what looked like dead silkworms were hanging from a metal framework supporting the roof of the larger room, we thought it might have been a silk factory at one time. The walls were covered with layers of old newspapers, probably for insulation against the chilling cold. We felt lucky that our regimental collecting station had been assigned to it since there were few other buildings in the area that hadn't been reduced to rubble.

"I'll bet you've set up shop in worse places," the man beside me said, as he took off his mittens. He tucked them under his arm, and then, like I was doing, tried to warm his hands over a little gasoline fired heater. The multiple layers of clothing he was wearing made his field jacket a tight fit.

"You've got that right, Major," I replied, remembering all too well the problems we had a month earlier with the viciously subzero winter weather far up in North Korea. "That was one bitch of a trip coming up here."

"Yeah," the Major replied, "thanks to that damned road bring so iced up."

"It really wasn't much over 30 kilometers," I said.

"Are they really pushing all that new metric stuff on us?"

"Well, we sort of do it both ways. It's supposed to be meters and kilometers, but we still sort of unofficially use yards and miles."

"More damned crap for me to learn," he said.

"If you remember that 50 miles equals 80 kilometers, you'll be okay."

"Just so our litter jeep and ambulance drivers can figure it out," the Major replied. He fished a package of cigarettes out of a pocket. As he lit one, he said, "I sure hope those Chinese that chased you guys out of North Korea will take their own sweet time about coming down here after you."

"Oh, they'll be here soon enough," I said, "even if they do have to walk."

The major shook his head. "You were lucky to survive all that shit."

I nodded. "Some of our medical officers didn't. That's how come I was transferred here."

"Aw, it was a goofy idea for old Dug Out Doug MacArther to send you guys up into North Korea," said Lt. Ramirez, one of our recently arrived dental officers. "He couldn't understand that the Chinese really meant what they said about coming into the war if we got too far north."

"Maybe he was getting bad advice from general fuck-ups on his staff at Eighth Army," I replied.

Ramirez laughed. "I haven't heard anybody say anything good about him."

"I don't mind saying," the Major said, "that when I hear you guys talking about all this stuff, I feel pretty damned inadequate. Just being chief of the surgical section of an Army base hospital sure as hell doesn't help much when it comes to running a collecting station. At least, the Captain here got some experience the hard way while he was in a battalion aid station."

I shrugged. "When I got here seven months ago, I hardly knew shit from Shinola about being a combat medic."

"Christ," Ramirez said, "who would have thought that those bastards in Washington would get us into another fucking war so soon!"

A tall, thin officer joined us at the stove and lit a cigarette. The ranking Medical Service Corps officer, he was one of the old hands who had also survived the disaster in North Korea and was in charge of all the non-medical aspects of running the collecting station.

After he blew out the match, he said, "Major Sloan, how do you want to set up? Your guys ought to be thawed out enough by now to do something useful."

The Major laughed. "Well, Captain Howard, why don't you ask my buddy here? He's the guy who understands all this shit."

"In a pig's ass," I said, as I finished loading my pipe and lit it. "Okay, the officers can bunk up in the smaller of the other two rooms, and the NCO medics in the larger one. The med techs can put their sleeping bags on litters in here if they haven't got cots. When casualties come in at night nobody will be sleeping."

Howard nodded. "Supply, Motor Pool and all our other sections should have their tents up by now."

"Your people did a great job of breaking in all your replacements while you were down in Chechon," I said.

"Yeah," Howard replied, "in spite of their bitching ."

"This setup is a hell of a lot better than anything we had when we were asshole deep in snow up north," I replied. "We better enjoy it while we can."

Lt. Weill, the other dentist, somewhat shorter than the rest of us, his bundled up clothing making him look even chubbier, said, "I never did give a shit about camping out."

"Don't worry," I answered. "We'll all be living in the tents soon enough."

"I just hope all these new guys know how to erect them," said Howard. "Seeing as how so many seem to be from the peacetime army, they probably only know about living in permanent barracks."

Sloan laughed. "Maybe that's one reason why they're bitching so much."

"You don't have to learn to bitch in this God-forsaken country," I said. "It comes naturally."

Sloan nodded. "Are the cooks getting organized, Bob?"

"Yeah, pretty much," he replied. "They've got their tent set up right next to this building. They like to put their field ranges outdoors because they're gasoline-fired. Lunch chow should be ready pretty soon."

Weill grunted. "Whatever they cook, it's got to be better than C-rations."

"Amen to that," Sloan replied. "I've had enough of them to last me forever."

"Where did they dig the latrine trench?" I asked. "It should be as far away from the mess as possible."

Howard nodded, as he replied, "Jones is supposed to have some of his Motor Pool people working on it as soon as they get all of their vehicles parked."

As he spoke, another man, stamping his feet, joined us at the little stove. Ed Jones, the Motor Pool officer, was rather short and swarthy and, unlike the rest of us, always seemed cheerful.

He fished a cigarette out of a pocket, and said, "Captain, we've already got the latrine ditch dug on the other side of this building. It sure wasn't easy. The fucking dirt is frozen so damned hard the guys had to use picks to break it up."

"It's about time," said Howard.

"Sounds like a good place for it," I commented. I couldn't help but notice how Jones' words, bland as they were, seemed to annoy Howard. Since it had only been two days since I had been transferred to this outfit, I hadn't had enough time yet to figure out how the personalities of the officers meshed, or clashed.

Jones lighted his cigarette. "It should be pretty well protected from cross winds, Captain. That's damned important when it's this cold and you're squatting over the ditch with your pants down."

I asked Howard, "Will we be getting in casualties any time soon?"

He shook his head. "I doubt it. Our battalions are still digging in a little ways north of town, sort of in blocking positions behind the other regiments that are dug in up near Hoensong. Their patrols don't to have hit much so far."

"Yeah," I said glumly, "but if the Chinese decide to knock out that ROK division on our right flank, the shit could really hit the fan."

"I can't figure out why anyone in their right mind would want this crappy town," Jones said. "There's almost nothing left of it."

Lighting a cigarette, Howard replied. "While it may not look like much of a town now, it's still at the juncture of five important supply routes, as well as having the northernmost railroad station left on the main line down to Pusan. It's important, all right."

Sloan said, "You guys sure don't seem to think much of those South Korean Army outfits."

"Are they really as undependable as I've been hearing?" Ramirez put in, as he lit a cigarette.

"Well, most of those outfits don't seem to be too well trained," I replied. "They aren't equipped anything like our people are. However, a couple of their divisions over to the east are said to be pretty good."

"By the way," Howard said, "when Charley Morse gets in from Division Rear this afternoon, he'll be bringing the Navy doc that's going to take over White Battalion's aid station."

Jones asked, "How come they're sending us a Navy doc?"

"It's because we don't have enough Army medical officers," Howard replied, almost as if he was addressing a child.

Of course, I realized that it would be up to me to see to it that our new medical officer from the Navy was properly oriented. I hoped that Morse, the service and supply company officer, and the only Medical Service Corps officer in the Collecting Station besides Howard who was a captain, would do a lot of the cluing in on the way.

After the medical equipment was finally all set up in the larger room, we set up our folding cots in the smaller room, inflated our air mattresses, and unrolled our Arctic sleeping bags on them. Another little gasoline-fired heater was lit, and soon took at least some of the bite out of the cold. There were problems with the car batteries used by our electric lighting system, so pending getting them recharged, after dark we would have to depend on our gasoline-fired Coleman lanterns.

CHAPTER 2

Just before evening chow, and as it was starting to get dark, Charley Morse arrived from Division Rear. I went out to help the Navy medical officer with his gear as, half frozen, he stiffly climbed out of the open jeep while clouds of steam arose from the exhaust pipe.

I showed the officer the way to our quarters. After he parked his gear on an unfolded canvas cot, he went straight to the little heater, and hopped up and down from one foot to the other as he tried to warm up and get his circulation going. I introduced Lt. Henry Marshall to the other rather curious officers and took the time to explain that his rank as a lieutenant in the Navy was equivalent to that of a captain in the Army.

He was dressed the same as the rest of us in standard Army issue combat clothing, except that while he had a regular steel helmet with his gear, he was wearing a pile arctic cap while we were all wearing our helmets. They were essentially two piece affairs, the steel helmet itself fitting snuggly over a helmet liner, which was plastic shell shaped just like the steel part. It could be worn separately as a sun or rain hat. Like the rest of us, he was bundled up in "long john" underwear, an olive drab woolen shirt and trousers, a sweater, greenish cotton twill field pants over the trousers, and a buttoned-up field jacket.

His boots were sturdy laced-up high-top shoes made of light colored leather with the rough side out, somewhat like suede. Puttee-like leather tops extended well up above the ankles and were fastened by two buckled leather straps, one above the other, on the outsides of the boots. His cotton twill field pants were bloused over his boots by being tucked up under rubber bands between the two straps, the way we all did it, although we often used the condoms in our medical supplies when we didn't have any rubber bands handy.

Like most officers, he was wearing a pistol belt around his waist with a holstered .45 caliber automatic pistol on the right side, and a quart-sized canteen in a canvas carrying case on the left. His pile Arctic cap with the ear flaps hanging down looked something like an aviator's helmet. It could be worn under a helmet liner. With the earflaps and the visor folded up, it somewhat resembled a Russian fur hat. He also was wearing the standard issue wool mittens, which had "fingers" for both the thumb and the first finger so that the wearer could pull a trigger. Leather gloves could be worn over the wool mittens.

His naval medical officer's branch of service badge was worn on the left side of his woolen shirt collar. On the right side of his collar was his naval lieutenant's badge of rank. Composed of two parallel silver bars, it was similar to an Army captain's badge of rank, the two, of course, being comparable. Pinned on his arctic cap's upturned visor was another rank badge. The rest of us were wearing our badges of rank and branch of service on the undersides of our field jacket lapels, with no insignia on artic caps or helmets, something that officers in combat units started doing very early in the war. Visible officers' rank badges, we soon learned, made good targets for enemy snipers.

The last to shake the lieutenant's hand was Major Sloan, who said, "Welcome to the war, Lieutenant. Glad to have you with us."

"Thanks, Major. Christ on a purple crutch, how long does this godforsaken country stay this damned cold?"

"Spring will come," I said. "It was hotter and more humid than a son of a bitch last summer. That's also when they have the monsoon rains and everything turns into mud."

"Crappy damned place," Marshall replied. "When we were coming over on the ferry boat from Japan, we could smell it before we could even see it."

I nodded. "They say that smell is a combination of coal smoke, the stuff the natives use to season food called kimchee, and the human shit they use for fertilizer. It's not so bad now when everything's frozen."

Charley Morse came in to stand around the stove with us, and said, "I can see that you bastards are already bullshitting the lieutenant with all your knee-length steel helmet stories."

"Hell, I'm impressed by how cheerful you guys seem to be," Marshall said. "The officers running the field medicine indoctrination course that we all had to take back in the States were a bunch of real sad sacks."

"Maybe that was because they really understood the situation," said Sloan.

"At least, Henry, you'll already have a few clues about running your battalion aid station," I said. "Anyhow, the MSC officer who'll be your assistant has been with the battalion ever since it got here last summer."

"Oh, hell," Marshall replied, "this is probably not much different than being stuck in a Navy medical outfit supporting the Marines. A lot of us who were in the Navy V-12 program are being called up and shipped over here for duty with them as well as with you people."

"Like the Army Specialized Training Program that I was in," I said. It was quite similar to the Navy V-12 program during World War II. These programs, somewhat controversial at the time, were established in 1943. Since men were being drafted down to eighteen years of age, it became recognized that they didn't have much time to get any college education while still civilians. To help insure a continuous supply of technically and professionally trained men to be officer candidates, qualified recruits were sent to colleges and universities all over the United States.

When that war ended, some of the men in the programs had completed pre-medical college training. After discharge from the military, they went on to graduate from medical school and subsequent internships under the GI Bill. Many of them, like me, also signed up in the military reserves, because it brought each of us a much-appreciated monthly stipend, along with a reserve officer's commission. Coming out of our internships just as the Korean War broke out, we instantly became available to be called to active duty as medical officers. Perhaps the government was already getting back its' money's worth.

Marshall asked, "Is this the division that has the all-black regiment?"

"No," I replied. "That's in another division where they're apparently having godawful problems. There's also an all black battalion."

"I never even heard of that," Marshall replied.

"That's probably because it's such a good one," Sloan said as, without ceremony, he fished a bottle of Scotch out of his barracks bag. We all promptly broke out the canteen cups that were nested around the canteens carried in the canvas cases on our pistol belts, and had a couple of drinks before dinner.

There were two large doors at the far end of the building, probably where trucks once were loaded. The cooks had opened them up and set up their mess tent and their hissing field ranges in the space so created.

We all brought our mess kits. Standard GI issue, they were essentially two oblong divided metal bowl-like pans that were hinged together and when folded up carried metal knives, forks and spoons inside. We unfolded them and removed the metal cups from around our canteens. As we worked out way down the chow line, the cooks dished out Vienna sausages, reconstituted mashed potatoes with gravy, canned grapefruit slices, and then filled our canteen cups with hot black coffee.

We then went back to our quarters and sat on our cots while we ate. When we were through, we took our mess kits and canteen cups back to the cooks' area to dip and swish them around in large garbage cans full of hot water heated by gasoline-fired units in order to clean and sterilize them. The mess did have dishes for the officers, but no one wanted to go to the bother of unpacking them.

Sloan found another bottle, and after we had a few more drinks, we were all in the sack by 2000, or 10:00 PM civilian time. As I began to shut down the Coleman lantern, I realized that amongst all the pages of Korean and Japanese newspapers plastered on the wall above my cot, there was also the front page from the September 12, 1948 issue of the *Los Angeles Times*.

As 1950 very quietly turned into 1951, I realized that I hadn't heard anyone say anything about a happy new year.

CHAPTER 3

While the next day dawned sunny and bright, it was very cold. After breakfast, Corporal Albert Gonzales, one of our drivers, and also a survivor of the Kunu-ri disaster, brought up a jeep with the litter racks folded up. I helped Lt. Marshall pile his gear on the back seat and climbed in after it while he settled into the front passenger's seat.

It was only a mile or so down a road bordered by ruined buildings to where a battalion medical aid station was set up in a native house. It was one of the few houses in Wonju that had suffered only surprisingly minimal damage. Near the entrance to the house, they had erected their "command post" tent that had a double draped sort of entrance that could be used during black-outs and not spill any light as people went in and out.

The tent could hold two unfolded litters set up on both sides of the tent with their handles supported by medical chests, leaving a narrow passage between them. There was also enough room for the aid station's other medical chests and equipment. Their 3/4 ton Dodge truck, a kind often called a "Weapons Carrier," was parked beside the tent, along with two litter jeeps, with their racks to carry litters extended. Not far away were the tents and vehicles of what I supposed was the 2nd Battalion headquarters.

We had no sooner stopped and climbed out of the jeep when a stocky man, stooping as he pushed aside the army blanket functioning as the door of the native house, came

Success to Stalemate in South Korea

forth to greet us. I recognized him as Lt. Mike Hayes, an MSC officer who was the assistant battalion surgeon.

"Hiya, Captain," he said. "Glad to see you guys, even if we are out of booze."

I laughed. "We finished off ours last night. Meet your new battalion surgeon, Navy Lieutenant Henry Marshall. Henry, this is Lt. Mike Hayes. He'll be your assistant to take care of all the non-medical stuff."

Hayes looked at Marshall's Navy insignia badges for a brief moment, and put out his gloved hand. "Pleased to meet you, Lieutenant. I did hear that we would be getting a Navy doc."

"Henry is one of the first," I said. Marshall seemed a bit hesitant, then I realized that he had noticed that Hayes, like the rest of us, was not wearing any visible insignia of rank or branch of service.

"Yeah," Marshall said. "It's because you guys have run out of Army docs."

Indeed, a Medical Collecting Station, a regimental level outfit, was supposed to be commanded by a medical officer in the rank of Major. There would then be two medical officers, who were Captains like me, under him, and who would supervise and work with the enlisted GI medical techs for the provision of medical care. However, we only had me, and I knew that there was little chance that we would be getting in another similar medical officer very soon.

For supervising all the service and supply operations that supported the operations of the Collecting station and the three Battalion Aid Stations, we had Medical Service Corps officers, usually who, while not doctors, had had first aid medical tech training. They supervised the non-medical activities that supported the operation of the collecting station and the battalion aid stations including personnel management, the motor pool and the drivers, supply services, the mess cooks and the troops assigned to establishing the bivouac areas including putting up and striking our tents.

In all, on the rosters of the collecting station and the three battalion aid stations were nearly 200 officers and men. An ambulance platoon, about six to eight ambulances headquartered at Division, was assigned to us for transporting patients from the Collecting station to the Division-level Clearing stations.

The Battalion Aid Stations, in turn, usually had a medical officer in charge who was a Captain. An MSC officer, a 1st Lieutenant, also trained as a medic, handled the non-medical support functions. The total number of officers and men in the aid station would be about 30. Collecting might also be medically supporting attached medical units in regimental level outfits such as artillery and tanks. Not unexpectedly, the system was really quite flexible.

We followed Hayes, who had picked up Marshall's gear, into the house, remembering to duck as we passed under the low lintel of the front door. Inside the smallish room a couple of cots with rolled–up sleeping bags on them had been set up. There were also some litters on the floor, some still folded and others opened. A folding desk had been set up with a field telephone placed on it. Hissing busily close by was a little gasoline heater. Electric lights were hanging down from the low ceiling, the bulbs looking a lot like sealed beam auto headlight units.

"We live in here," said Hayes, as he set Marshall's gear down. "It's easier to keep warm in here than in the Command Post tent."

"That's where you see patients?" I asked.

"Right. Putting some of our stuff in here gives us a lot more room when we're working there."

"Are your people seeing any action?"

Hayes shook his head. "No, but our line companies are already getting into position and digging in. They should start their patrolling up towards Hoensong by tomorrow. Some outfits up there have already reported seeing what they think are Chinese reconnaissance patrols. That's only about ten miles from here."

"I hope you'll have enough time to show the Lieutenant around and get him properly oriented," I said, as I looked at my watch. "Well, Henry, what do you think of your new home away from home?"

Marshall lit a cigarette as he looked around the cluttered room. "I guess it's better than I thought it would be. At least, it's passably warm in here. I thought I might be living ass-deep in a snow-filled foxhole."

"We try to be as comfortable as possible," Hayes replied. "First, I'll get you to remove your badges and put them under the lapels of your field jacket where they won't attract the attention of gook snipers. They like to pick off the officers first. Our medics don't wear Red Cross armbands for the same reason."

Marshall took off his steel helmet and scratched his head. "Well, then, how can you tell the officers from the enlisted men?"

"We just have to figure it out. Officers in combat outfits won't even wear identifying white stripes on the backs of their helmets. Some won't even wear .45 automatics, because the gooks know that GIs wearing them are likely to be officers. Instead, they'll carry a carbine or maybe a rifle, just like the GIs."

Marshall turned to me and said, "You guys in Collecting don't seem to be wearing any unit insignia, either."

I laughed, if without much humor. "Even though we're usually not quite as close to the enemy as the rifle companies and the battalion aid stations, we're still close enough to get shot at by gook infiltrators."

Marshall nodded, and then asked, "Can any of you people tell me why you call the North Koreans and even the Chinese 'gooks?'"

"Well," I answered, "as I understand it, it's because the Korean word for 'man,' or 'gentleman,' is 'gook.' For example, an American is a 'megook,' a Chinese is a 'chungook,' a South Korean is a 'hangook,' and a North Korean is an 'inmungook.'" The 'gook' part is what seems to have stuck in the GI heads."

Hayes laughed. "I've also heard that the troops say things like "north gooks, south gooks samo samo."

"Maybe," I said, "that's because they're so pissed off about being sent here."

Hayes lighted a cigarette, and as he turned to me, he said, "Have you told him about the KATUSAs?"

"KATUSAs?" Marshall looked puzzled.

I had to laugh. "No, I guess I haven't. Henry, they're South Korean soldiers that have been sent to us as replacements because we were getting in so few of them in from the States. "KATUSA" is an acronym for 'Korean Augmentation to the US Army.' "

"Yeah," Hayes said, "they're too short for GI uniforms, their feet don't fit GI boots, and they all get belly aches on GI food."

"The idea was to send them out mostly to line companies where the GIs could train them," I said. "It doesn't seem to have worked as well as was hoped."

"Some of them are doing okay," Hayes replied. "It's hard to communicate with them in technical terms because of the language barrier. They seem to function better when they're together in groups of their own people. Some divisions refuse to have anything to do with them. However, our outfits have managed to train some of them to be pretty good riflemen."

Marshall shook his head "How do you handle them on sick call?"

"We get the houseboys to translate."

"Aren't they KATUSAs?"

Hayes shook his head. "No, we pay them. They're not in the ROK army. Hell, they sign up with us as houseboys to avoid being drafted into it. The KATUSAs get paid by the ROK army."

"We don't have nearly as many as we used to, now that we're getting in more replacements from the States," I said, as I checked my watch. "Maybe it's time for me to get rolling."

As I turned to leave, Hayes grinned, and said, "Please don't leave, Captain, until you clue me in about any good rumors you've heard lately."

I laughed. Rumors seemed to be something akin to life-blood of the Army. "Well, Cpl. Gonzalez here reported that one of the truck drivers from Division told him that he had heard that Eighth Army is talking about setting up a rest and recuperation plan in Japan for the combat troops."

"No shit?" said Hayes. "I've also heard that our division is going to be transferred into X Corps."

Gonzalez nodded. "That's one's almost for damned sure."

Hayes frowned, and then turning to me, he said, "That's the Corps the GIs call the ass-less army because they don't like its top brass. It could also mean that we might be having the Marine division with us. They hate that Corps' brass even more than we do."

"I guess that could also mean that they'll soon be having us going on the offensive," I replied, "rather than just sitting around and waiting for the gooks to come down here after us."

"Wouldn't doubt it at all," Hayes replied. "All okay back at Collecting?"

"As well as can be expected," I replied.

Hays nodded. "Is Howard still riding Jones' ass?"

"Not that I know of," I said, shaking my head. "Why should he?"

Hayes pitched the extinguished match away. "Aw, he seems to get more than a little pissed at times with Jones. The guy can get out of order when there's any booze around, like when the regimental whisky rations come in. Maybe there's more to it than just that. Jones doesn't seem to like Howard much, either."

I laughed. "Well, we haven't had a whisky ration lately."

Hayes took off his helmet and scratched his head. "Maybe the troops will have to get their kicks from taking benzedrine."

"Taking benzedrine?" Marshall asked, a bit aghast.

"Sure," I said. "We used hell of a lot of it up in North Korea. After the Chinese came into the war, the troops had to run over those goddamned mountains all day changing positions while we tried to retreat. Then, everybody had to stay awake all night fighting the Chinese."

"Couldn't guys in the line outfits take turns with each other?"

"Christ," Hayes said, "we were taking so many casualties, the line outfits didn't have enough able-bodied men left to take turns. We couldn't even let the poor bastards have their Arctic sleeping bags at night for fear they'd doze off."

"A couple of outfits got over-run by the Chinese because their outposts did just that," I added.

"Being so goddamned cold was a hell of a problem," Hayes added.

I nodded. "It got down to something like 20 degrees or more below zero every goddamned night."

"You guys are beginning to scare the shit out of me," Marshall grunted.

"Well," I answered, "things are a lot different. Our outfits are getting pretty much up to strength and are a lot better equipped. The gooks will be the ones with the long supply lines now."

"I'll see to it that he gets clued in," Hayes said.

CHAPTER 4

Gonzales started up the jeep to head back to Collecting as I climbed into the passenger's seat. As we drove along, he said, "Captain, I'll bet that most of these new replacements we're getting in have no fuckin' idea at all about what it was like up there in North Korea."

I nodded. "To them, it's probably all just ancient history."

Needless to say, I wished that I could be assigned to a clearing station, the next stop back on the evacuation route for casualties after the collecting station. However, docs assigned to clearing stations were supposed to have at least some formal surgical training, and I had been just out of my internship when I had been rushed to South Korea the previous July. Still, being assigned to a regimental collecting station was a sort of a promotion and better duty than being in an infantry battalion aid station.

It was noticeable that the truck traffic was building up, suggesting that a lot more troops were being brought into the area. As we neared Collecting, I saw a C-47 transport plane taking off from an unpaved airstrip not 300 meters away. I could also see that a combat engineer outfit was busily working on the south end of the airstrip with their heavy equipment, undoubtedly to lengthen it so that it would be able to handle larger transport aircraft. Considering the poor roads in the area, the reports of possible enemy guerilla activity in the surrounding countryside, and the prospect of worsening winter weather, I realized that we might have to depend on drops from aircraft for our supplies.

After lunch in Collecting's mess, Ed Jones picked up a litter jeep with a folded up litter rack from our motor pool and drove me to an ROK surgical hospital on the far eastern side of Wonju. It seemed very crude, and smelled evilly of fish. I could only guess at what the place would be like when they were receiving casualties.

Then, we stopped by the division clearing station on the south side of the town that was backing us up. Since we would be evacuating our casualties to it, I wanted to make sure that they knew where our collecting station was bivouacked.

That afternoon, I lectured the new aid men about how we treated sick call as well as casualties. I also mentioned that not only did we receive sick men and battle casualties from the battalion aid stations, they would often also send in GIs with bizarre complaints and leave it to us in Collecting to decide whether they were for real. Then, we had to do the stiff-arming of sending the ones we were sure were malingerers back to duty.

It was the next day, the second of the New Year, when we began seeing patients, many of them very unhappy new replacements that had just arrived. We split our medics into two shifts, one for the morning and afternoon, the other for the evening and night. Sometimes they would all have to be on duty at the same time, depending on the casualty flow.

The medics, or "aid men," out with the line companies would administer first aid to the wounded by bandaging them as best they could to control bleeding, even applying tourniquets if bleeding from wounds in extremities could not be otherwise controlled. They would also give morphine injections to control pain and tie a field medical tag to the casualty's clothing, listing his injuries, and how much morphine or other medications he had been given.

If the wounded were unable to walk, litter bearers, or sometimes other GIs, would then carry them out on litters. They would then be loaded on jeeps equipped with litter racks. The litter jeeps would then carry the wounded back to the battalion aid stations. Too often, the poor Korean dirt roads limited speeds to little more than 15 miles an hour. Depending on circumstances, distances back to the aid stations could be a just few hundred yards or even a mile or so.

In the battalion medical aid stations, the bandages would be tidied up, and splints to support and stabilize leg and arm injuries applied. The medical officer would check the patient's condition and direct the medics in how to treat them. Plasma could be started intravenously to temporarily replace blood volume loss, since if it got too low, the patient could go into shock as important organs would start to shut down. Tourniquets to control bleeding had to be checked since they had to be released periodically to avoid damage to remaining uninjured tissue.

Emergency tracheostomies, where facial and neck wounds blocked adequate air flow to the lungs, were occasionally done by battalion surgeons. The procedure involved making a surgical opening in the trachea, the "wind pipe" in the front of the neck, and inserting a plastic tube to keep the airway open.

More morphine could be given to control pain. Some minor cleaning of wounds and trimming could be done where absolutely necessary, although the main idea was to get the seriously wounded evacuated as quickly as possible to facilities where more comprehensive care would be available. Penicillin by intramuscular injection was routinely administered. The drug was so new then that we didn't have to worry about any of the wounded being allergic to it. What was done was noted on the casualty's field medical tag, or "FMT,"

From the battalion aid station, the patients were evacuated, again by litter jeeps, to the regimental collecting station, also located anywhere from a few hundred yards to a mile or so further back, depending on the situation. The medical officers would assess the individual patient's condition and direct what had to be done to be sure that they were stabilized and supervise the medics while they checked bandages, splints and tourniquets. More plasma could be administered if necessary, splints adjusted, and penicillin injections given if it hadn't been in the battalion aid station. Keeping the wounded as warm as possible in the wintertime was mandatory.

Men with short duration illnesses such as colds, ear and throat infections, and gastroenteritis could sometimes be treated and kept for a few days in the collecting station, and then returned to duty. FMTs were made out for them, just as it was done for those sent further back, and duly recorded. It was not unusual, however, for GIs to feign or exaggerate their symptoms, in the hope that they would be evacuated much further to the rear and, with luck, somehow never be returned to a line outfit.

After all, it was a war being fought in a most undesirable far away place for reasons that the vast majority of American soldiers could not understand. However, once the GIs saw the barbarous way that the North Korean and Chinese armies treated their prisoners, their resolve tended to become significantly stiffened.

The wounded would then be sent on to a Division Clearing Station, usually in "crackerbox" ambulances. They got the name from their box-like bodies that could accommodate four casualties on litters. Sometimes it was a distance of only a few miles or so, or occasionally, depending on circumstances, much further. At the Clearing station, more definitive care was available as well as emergency surgery and live-saving whole blood transfusions.

As soon as possible, the casualties would then be sent further on back to a well-equipped Mobile Army Surgical Hospital unit for more definitive care. They were often positioned near a railroad when possible. After the wounded were treated they would be evacuated by trains to hospitals set up farther south and, depending on the severity of their wounds, even on to Japan.

Too often, particularly early in the war, MASH units had to be kept many miles to the rear because of the generally unstable lines of battle. Indeed, there was a cynical one-liner going around amongst the GIs to the effect that if you could survive being evacuated to a MASH, you would probably be able to survive anything they could do to you when you finally got there.

A real problem that we had was with the morphine. It was contained in little squeezable tubes with hollow needles, called syrrets. While the aid men would usually swab off an injection site on the upper arms with alcohol before administering the morphine, often, particularly in the winter, they would simply plunge the needle of the syrrets right through the clothing. The amount of morphine the syrrets contained was nearly twice the dose commonly used in ordinary civilian practice. With lowering blood volume due to hemorrhaging, the pick-up of morphine from the peripheral injection sites was minimized. As a wounded man continued to complain of pain while being transported, particularly on those often so-slow runs on very poor roads between medical facilities, more shots of morphine might be given. When his blood volume, as he received plasma intravenously, started to rise, more of the morphine in the injection sites could be picked up, with the possibility of it all adding up to a dangerous over-dose. Proper recording of morphine shots on the field medial tags was supposed to help avoid this.

We tried to train our medical corpsmen to evaluate how much pain a wounded man was having, and if appropriate, squeeze out perhaps half the contents of the syrrets before injecting the rest. While it was well understood even then that pain significantly contributed to shock, and must be relieved, the problem was in trying to give just enough of the opiate drug to satisfactorily control the pain without overdoing it.

We also were seeing problems with feet, beyond the problems with frostbite. While every effort was made to provide the GIs with well-fitting boots, sometimes it didn't work out that way, particularly for the men with bigger feet. They would often suffer abrasions sometimes as well as blisters. The treatment was soaking the affected feet in a potassium permanganate solution. This was often done by using their steel helmets as bowls, if there weren't any better sized native bowls available. It did seem to work, although toenails assumed a purple color that seemed to last indefinitely.

Our battalions began more aggressive patrolling, and soon were encountering small groups of North Koreans and Chinese well south of Hoensong. Because they would usually try to slip away without fighting, they were thought to be reconnaissance parties. To the east and south of us our patrols were running into what were presumed to be bands of guerillas composed mostly of North Koreans left behind during their hurried retreat to the north during the previous September and October.

That night we were very busy, as the action on the front lines started to heat up. Not only were there battle casualties, but also a few GIs whose wounds we were pretty sure were self-inflicted, despite the often rather fanciful explanations about how they happened. A soldier from the Netherlands battalion that had just been attached to one of our regiments and was involved in the fighting north of us was brought in with abdominal pains and was also evacuated.

The three regimental chaplains were kept busy dealing with soldiers who were new to combat and had personal problems. I wondered if the chaplains' duty was basically, when all was said and done, much the same as ours as medical officers, which, put simply, was to do the best we could to keep as many of the troops as possible on the firing line.

Things didn't calm down until well after midnight. We were certainly back in the war. And indeed, the fighting soon became even more intense. A company-sized patrol from one of our other infantry battalions further to the north mistook an estimated battalion-sized group of North Koreans for friendly ROK soldiers and was soon nearly surrounded. The GIs finally managed to fight their way out but only after a prolonged running battle in deep snow.

There was increasing pressure on our division's other two regiments still dug in just south of Hoensong. There was also a real concern that a large number of the enemy might have already infiltrated between some of our forward rifle company positions and could soon be threatening the ROK division on our right flank. A major offensive to take Wonju by the Chinese Communist Forces and the reconstituted, by the Russians, units of the previously defeated North Korean Peoples Army was clearly under way.

We began to see more and more refugees along the roads as they fled southward ahead of the communist armies. Initially a trickle, it soon became something like a flood. Division MPs tried to keep them from blocking roads, but it was difficult.

CHAPTER 5

The Division engineer battalion continued to work day and night to extend the nearby unpaved airstrip, but was now running into difficulties clearing a wide enough gap through a large berm of frozen earth at the south end of it. It was probably piled up when the runway was first scraped out of the frozen soil. Our trucks were being kept busy hauling combat troops around Wonju to establish defensive positions. On the 3rd, we had an airdrop of 250 tons of sorely needed supplies on the airstrip from low-flying L-119 cargo aircraft. Most of the supplies seemed to be drums of gasoline. The airstrip was still too short for the L-119s to land, much less take off.

Despite the increasing fighting to the north and west, the battalions in our regiment did not seem to be having a lot of casualties. I was able to briefly visit the medical officer who was assigned to the aid station in Division Forward several miles to the rear and south of Wonju. He told me that he was able to confirm that there was indeed talk of a new R and R plan in Japan beginning with those of us who had first arrived in the war, although he knew nothing of the details. As minimal as the information was, it was at least somewhat reassuring.

In the midst of our increasing anxieties about the enemy's intentions, our division's commanding general, in what almost predictably proved to be a controversial attempt to improve morale, issued an edict to the effect that all of us in the division should start to grow facial hair. Each regiment and attached units would do it a little differently. One unit would grow goatees, another sideburns, a third mustaches, a fourth full beards, and so on. While the general was quite popular with the GIs in the ranks, we still had to wonder a little about the propriety of all this facial hair business. After all, we weren't wearing any visible identifying insignia, such as Division shoulder patches or badges of rank and branch of service.

We were kept busy until well after midnight seeing battle casualties, not so much from our regiment's three battalions, but from other outfits as the situation further to the north deteriorated and became more urgent. Also, we were seeing more and more forlorn GIs with weird complaints that were clearly the result of fear of facing combat. It almost seemed as if the GIs who had survived the terrors of the Kunu-ri debacle a little over a month previously, and had now been assigned back into line rifle companies, were the ones more likely to show up on sick call than even the poorly motivated new replacements.

On the morning of the 5th of January, we were up early and in the mess area for breakfast. There wasn't much of the usual jocularity. Even the cooks were worried, and I noticed that they had their gear pretty much packed up as if they were getting ready to move out at a moment's notice. This meant that breakfast was mainly cereal that came in little boxes that were lined with waxed paper and could be slit open and used as bowls by pouring in reconstituted powdered milk. We also had fried bacon, bread, and coffee.

"Well," Major Sloan said, "it looks like there's big trouble ahead of us."

"I've heard it said," I replied, "that if your ass is starting to pucker, you're beginning to understand the situation."

"You've got that right, Doc," said Howard. "Remember, I was in a battalion aid station in the South Pacific, and mine sure is twitching now."

Charley Morse came in and poured a cup of coffee. "Maybe we better start packing up and loading everything so we can hyaku the hell out of here in a hurry. We could be in deep shit if we don't get our trucks back damned soon."

"What makes you say that?" Sloan asked, as he lit a cigarette.

"I was just over at Regimental Supply. They say there are gooks all over the place up around Hoensong. Some outfits are having a bitch of a time trying to break contact and pull back."

"Hoensong isn't all that far away from here," I commented.

"That's for damned sure," said Howard. "Some of our six bys may still be up there hauling troops. We'll sure need them if we have to haul ass."

"Well, how in the hell do we get them back?" Sloan anxiously asked.

"Division is already bugging the bejesus out of Corps," Morse replied. "All of our outfits want their trucks back."

Howard stood up as he crushed out a cigarette. "Okay, Major, do I have your permission to start packing and loading up everything we can, so we can load our other trucks in a hurry as soon as they get back?"

"Hell, yes, Bob," said Sloan, also standing up. "Maybe you better even rout out the guys who were working late last night."

"How do we fit in?" asked Mario Ramirez, who with our other dental officer, Julian Weill, had remained silent so far.

Howard took of his steel helmet and scratched his head. "Well, it seems to me that you could be the most useful by supervising the guys who are not only packing up your dental gear, but getting it loaded. Is that okay, Major?"

Sloan nodded towards me and said, "The Captain here and I can look out for the packing and loading of our medical stuff by our medics. The MSC officers have their own outfits to look after."

Howard nodded. "I'll tell Jones to get up off his dumb ass and make sure the motor pool's packed up, and all our vehicles are gassed up, including the others as soon as they come back."

It all made sense. I had a lot to do, and for a moment again wished we had another medical officer like me in the Collecting station as was authorized. I also again wondered why Howard had so little good to say about Ed Jones.

"Incidentally, before you guys go," said Morse, "a supply train is supposed to be coming up any time now. I heard that it's been due for a week. They'll be rounding up everyone they can to help unload it in a hurry. They want to get it back down south before the gooks blow up the tracks somewhere."

"What military genius is responsible for that?" asked Sloan. "We just had that airdrop of supplies two days ago."

"Beats the shit out of me, Major," Morse replied. "Maybe it will at least help us get our trucks back sooner."

The supply train arrived in mid-morning, and was hurriedly unloaded with all available personnel pressed into the job so the train could quickly move back south. In the meantime, it was ominous that the numbers of refugees fleeing down the road near us seemed to be increasing.

CHAPTER 6

There was no question that the enemy had begun their long-awaited offensive. The rest of the collecting station was soon loaded on our errant trucks as soon as they rejoined us later that day. We kept out enough supplies in the back of a 3/4 ton truck parked close to the building to treat casualties as we impatiently awaited orders to move out. However, we had been seeing surprisingly few casualties. Considering what we were hearing about the near-desperate fighting that had erupted to the north, I wondered if it could mean that things might be getting chaotic enough to interfere with the evacuation of wounded.

It was often difficult to know exactly was happening out in our aid stations because of communication problems. Our SCR-300 radios, called "walkie-talkies" because the radio and the attached battery pack could be carried on a man's back, were mostly relics from World War II. Because their transmissions could be blocked by hilly terrain, we were often forced to rely on nearby tank and artillery outfits to convey urgent messages because they had better radios.

The field telephones that we mostly depended upon for linking us with our aid stations as well as the other units, such as regimental and battalion headquarters, depended on telephone wire put down along the sides of roads and paths by Signal Corps jeeps with large rotating reels of it. Every attempt was made to position the wires as far away from the sides of the roads as possible. This was to prevent vehicles from inadvertently tearing the wires out, usually when backing up to turn around, or simply turning off to the side. The tracked vehicles presented the greatest problems.

Line companies would often string telephone wire by hand out to their outposts, and even use said wires for guidance to forward positions at night, but they were easily displaced. Hand-held radios, called "handy-talkies," were often used by companies and their platoons, but their range was quite limited, usually to little more than the immediate company area.

When everything was quiet, there wasn't too much of a problem, but in the heat of battle our communication methods could often become uncertain. Reliance then had to be placed on the uncertain abilities of runner-couriers to convey important messages in the old fashioned way.

The CCF and NKPA had even more primitive ways of communication between their units. We knew that they had some radios, but they were rarely found below regimental level. If wire could be laid, they would have telephones to communicate with battalions, and they would also use flares shot into the sky. Bugles were commonly used at company level for signals, and whistles at platoon level. They needed to use such aural devices because they most often fought at night to avoid American aircraft observation and attacks. They also heavily relied on couriers at every level of command, and they reportedly had horses and mules to help.

Jittery young GIs, hunkered down in their frozen foxholes as they anxiously and fearfully waited for something to happen, often seemed to become more unnerved by the sounds of the enemy's signals, particularly the bugles, than they were by incoming gunfire. Indeed, a favorite method of attack by the Asian armies was to not fire weapons that would give away their presence while quietly sneaking up on the American lines in the dark.

We didn't have enough GIs to present a solid combat line, like in World War I with trenches. Instead, our wide combat fronts were usually set up as a series of fortified strong points placed as often as possible on higher ground. Protection of the terrain between them was attempted by registering weapons on the open spaces. Mines and ordnance with trip wires to catch enemy infiltrators in the dark of night were often used. However, the enemy was often clever enough to be able to sneak undetected through those gaps between the strong point positions. Their inverted V shaped marching formations often enabled them to silently envelope individual groups of GIs when it was dark. They could then suddenly shower the foxholes with grenades, and then rush the survivors from all sides and engage them in hand-to-hand combat. The thrown grenades would give little indication of which direction the attackers were coming from, making it hard for the GIs in the dark to know which way to shoot to repel them.

So, when the bugles and whistles sounded in the dark, frightened GIs in some outfits would too often be tempted to mindlessly "bug out" to the rear, as they feared an enemy attack, even if they didn't know from which direction.

CHAPTER 7

Late that afternoon, we learned that Division Forward had already pulled back to set up in the vicinity of Chungju, a distance of about 50 kilometers, or 30 miles. Just before dark, we were also finally ordered to immediately move back to the south. With everything else including our personnel already loaded on the waiting trucks, we were soon able to get on the road. Regimental Headquarters had already moved out just ahead of us.

We didn't have far to go as night fell, just a few miles, but the going was very slow, mostly in low gear and only occasionally in second, over a poor road that was still icy and often deep in snow. Our jeep driver had all he could handle trying to keep our jeep on the road even at such slow speeds. Also, we could only use our dim blackout headlights, which furnished little illumination during snow flurries. The reason for using them was to avoid, as much as possible, attracting the attention of guerillas that might be lurking nearby, as if they couldn't hear the sounds of our vehicles' laboring engines.

Despite the foul weather, there seemed to be ever more refugees plodding along the sides of the road as they tried to stay ahead of the again-invading communist forces. Tired as they must have been, they would often inadvertently wander out into the road ahead of our vehicles. They were often hard to see, because most of them were bundled up in light colored clothing. It was almost a miracle that, as far as we knew, we hadn't hit any of them.

Fortunately, the jeep in which Sloan, Howard and I were riding still had its removable top and side curtains, although it still was rather drafty. Many of our vehicles seemed to have lost their weather protection gear along the way, since it wasn't supposed to be used in combat situations where the windshields were to be folded flat on hoods.

When we finally reached our designated bivouac site near Regiment's new area, we were relieved that what we could see of it in the dark appeared to be a field that was reasonably flat. Expecting to soon be ordered to move on again, we decided to unpack and set up as few tents as possible for the night, mainly to just house our people. Putting up the clumsy canvas tents in the dark while it was snowing, with the temperature down to way below zero, was no easy task. Digging slit trenches for latrines in the frozen earth again required the use of pickaxes as well as shovels.

The enlisted medics took over two squad tents and the officers bedded down in one of the pyramidal tents. We didn't bother with the electric lights and depended on the gasoline-fired lanterns. They also helped the heaters take at least some of the edge off the cold. Dinner, of course, was from C-rations.

The lanterns had just been extinguished, when I heard one of the dentists yell out, "Hey there, Morse, what's your middle name?"

Bob Howard's voice boomed out, "Quit that shit, you crazy bastards!"

It was an old barracks gag. As they lay there in their bunks after lights out, one GI would yell out something like, "Hey there, Smith, what's your middle name?" If Smith answered, "William," then the first guy would yell back, "Well, fuck you, William!" It would go around like that until the rest of the men in the barracks tired of it and shouted down the questioners. They were probably just trying to be funny.

It seemed a little unusual, perhaps even juvenile, for a group of officers to behave this way, even though most of them were still in their twenties. The average age of the men in an Army infantry division, from the commanding general on down, would usually be about 21 years.

CHAPTER 8

We were continuing to see frostbite casualties, first noted when we were far up in North Korea in October and November 1950. A major cause was what were called "Shoe-pacs." They had been issued to take the place of the regular GI boots in the near arctic weather and often-deep snow. However, the Shoe-pacs were poorly ventilated, and in fact were specifically designed for even colder weather than what we had been experiencing, cold as it was. They had a top of horsehide, and a lower part and soles that were of a rubber-like material.

The problem was that, because of their lack of much ventilation, feet would begin to sweat as the men were walking in the snow, and then the sweat would tend to soon freeze in the sub-zero temperatures when the men stopped walking for whatever reason. The result, too often, could be the prompt onset of surprisingly severe frostbite.

To prevent this from happening, the GIs were expected to carry extra absorbable innersoles and were to rotate them with the ones in their Shoe-pacs as they became dampened. They were supposed to put the exchanged damp innersoles inside their clothing behind their belts and against their long john underwear to dry out. However, GIs sometimes lost their spares, and also, when in combat, they often were reluctant to take the time to stop and remove their boots in order to rotate the innersoles.

By the 6th of January, NKPA and CCF divisions were putting even more pressure on the embattled combat units from the other regiments of our division that were still trying to pull back from Hoensong towards Wonju. Continuing to be harried all the way by the enemy as they tried to withdraw in the deepening snow, they took increasing casualties.

We heard that they had to destroy the train that was still in Wonju. The enemy advance, driving to the southwest of us, as had been feared, threatened a wooden railroad bridge, recently constructed by the engineers, further down the railroad line towards Yoju. When attempts to blow it up failed, so the story went, the officer in charge chose to quickly soak the bridge with gasoline and set it on fire.

By later that night our division's line battalions had all been ordered to pull back and were digging in on higher and more defensible ground a few miles to the south of Wonju. Soon, the battered town was reported to be overrun by the enemy. We had to move back a few more kilometers to the south.

Although we heard that the division had been ordered to attack and retake Wonju, Collecting was again ordered to move even further to the south. The road was still cluttered by large groups of refugees who, in their desperation, still moved both by day and night, whatever the weather. That afternoon, one of our battalions guarding our main supply route, the road up towards Wonju, was hit by what was reported to be an enemy regiment. Despite taking casualties, our people fought off the Chinese and the MSR remained open. We later heard that Division's attempts to retake Wonju continued to be notably unsuccessful.

On the 9th of January, we again moved south, this time to near Chupo-ri, about 30 kilometers, or 20 miles, south of Wonju, and 4 kilometers west of Chechon. It was much flatter country, and several other army outfits were also bivouacked in the area. While the snow seemed ever deeper, the weather seemed to become a bit warmer, or was it less cold, than it had been further north. Our litter jeep drivers out with the battalion aid stations were hard put to keep up with our movements. It was extremely fortunate that the tortuous roads between the Battalion Aid Stations, the Collecting Station, and the Clearing station were otherwise fairly decent.

I soon discovered that another medical officer I knew from my internship year was assigned to the collecting station of a nearby infantry division. There was also a medical officer in a nearby field artillery battalion who had been a medical school classmate of mine. I felt considerably less persecuted after seeing that so many of my doctor contemporaries were also involved in the war.

Working in our tents had been challenging at first, but we soon adapted ourselves to it and our two-shift arrangement for aid personnel worked well. The major and I had a blackout tent, like the kind used by the battalion aid stations. The other officers had a pyramidal eight man tent. There was also a mess tent, much like the eight-man type. Our Motor Pool personnel had their tents, as did our Service and Supply people and those of our other support units. The Division-based ambulance drivers usually slept in their vehicles when they weren't evacuating patients. The collecting station took up a fair amount of area since we tried to keep everything well spread out as a defense against incoming artillery fire, or even possible enemy aerial attack.

Our vehicles were composed of jeeps equipped with racks for carrying litters, 3/4 ton trucks, and 2 1/2 ton 6x6 trucks. We also usually had several of the "crackerbox" ambulances assigned to us that were mechanically similar to our Dodge 3/4 ton trucks. While they were painted the same olive-drab color as our other vehicles, they also originally had large red crosses painted over a square white background on their sides. The enemy found those crosses to be great targets, so most of the ambulances soon had the crosses and white backgrounds covered up with hastily-applied olive drab paint. Almost all of these vehicles, as well as most of our other equipment, were of World War II vintage.

While we usually set up the collecting station near Regimental Headquarters, we were now situated closer to a Heavy Mortar outfit, so we made a deal to join our mess with theirs. The mess sergeant of the mortar outfit claimed that he had been in the division so long that he had been a sergeant when the present commanding general was still a second lieutenant leading a rifle company platoon. Since we had to put out guards around our perimeters at night because of the threat of guerilla activity, it was nice to have GIs from an actual combat outfit joining our people in manning the foxholes.

The first patients who came in after we were set up were more frostbite cases, and then one of the battalion aid stations sent in six GI's who apparently had been captured and then turned loose by North Korean guerillas operating in the area. They claimed that they had been treated well. Their story caused several curious war correspondents and even a general to come to visit us.

CHAPTER 9

Division's attempts to retake Wonju continued to be unsuccessful. We heard it rumored that the top brass of Eighth Army, as well as the Corps commander and the new theater commander, General Ridgeway, had become quite unhappy about the situation. The division's commanding general, of course, had to take the blame. A serious problem was that he not first gotten authorization from higher authority for the division to abandon Wonju in the first place, much less to retreat further to take up those positions on the higher ground south of it.

The next day, four young soldiers were brought in from one of the battalion aid stations with bullet holes in their left feet. Their explanations about how the wounds happened were too fanciful to be believed. We had no doubt that they were self-inflicted. However, proving what we surmised was very difficult because none of their buddies would ever admit to having seen them do it. This was becoming all too common.

Three times we tried to evacuate them to the division clearing station down near Chechon. The ambulance returned twice, the driver stating that there was a roadblock that had been set up, he thought, by stubborn guerillas. A patrol from the Heavy Weapons outfit finally took out the roadblock, and the ambulance was then able to get through. Later, another GI came in complaining of tuberculosis in

Success to Stalemate in South Korea

his feet. Examination was quite negative so we soon sent him back to duty.

The collecting station had to pack up again the next day and move to another location that was both more convenient to the road and more centrally positioned behind our regiment's three battalion aid stations. The little valley, under a six-inch mantle of new snow, seemed rather picturesque whenever the winter sun briefly managed to peak through the leaden, low-hanging clouds still clinging to the barren hilltops surrounding us. The weather otherwise was clear and dry, although the temperature would still drop precipitously at night to 20 below zero or more. I had to admit that there were times while I was going to medical school in the Middle West when it seemed to be nearly as cold.

I received a rather battered but intact package from home in the mail, the first in weeks. It contained a new pipe, handkerchiefs, underwear, a shaving mirror, cans of tortillas, and cheese. Mail had finally begun to arrive with some degree of regularity. It now took about two weeks to get to us from the US West Coast. With the aid of the little mirror, I was able to determine that my facial hair was now an eighth of an inch long.

That night, a couple of GIs from an infantry squad belonging to another regiment were brought in to the collecting station. They had been cut off from their outfit while trying to work their way back south towards Wonju a week previously. The men had been trudging south through deep snow for several days while dodging enemy patrols, when they met up with a young Korean male civilian, also a refugee, who offered to lead them out. He did so, while carrying a two-year old child on his back, and with his two sons that appeared to be about ages 12 and 14. He had used the two boys as scouts as he led the little group out over the hills and through the communist Chinese lines. We checked out the South Koreans as best we could, and saw to it that they had something to eat and a sheltered place to sleep. The little child had a cold, which we treated, and we did our best for the others. The two GIs had developed rather severe cases of frostbite and had to evacuated, along with their South Korean savior and his children.

The enemy was now reportedly beginning to withdraw some of its forces back to the north. It was also reported, rather surprisingly, that the CCF and the NKPA had suffered what was described as "staggering" losses. This unexpected turn of events was because many artillery units, some only recently arrived from the States, had been hurriedly brought up by Corps to support the beleaguered line outfits near Wonju. They also had effective air support.

Despite this success, the line units were again ordered by Division to begin pulling further back through the snow in order to consolidate a stronger line on even higher ground further south of Wonju. This also unauthorized order apparently proved to be the last straw for the High Command. Later the same day, we were not too surprised to hear that our commanding general had been rather summarily sacked. It was now becoming very apparent that the American forces were being far more capably commanded by General Ridgway than what had been the case previously under General MacArthur.

Since our outfits were beginning to experience less enemy contact, there were a few relatively quiet days for the collecting station. We were sure that it would not be long now before an order would be issued to all units to shave off the facial hair. Most of us would be quite happy to obey it.

CHAPTER 10

On January 16th, I was ordered to go back to Division Rear, now located near Miryang, nearly 120 miles, or about 190 kilometers, to the south. The only personnel records that Division had been able to take with them during the hurried retreat from Pyongyang after the Chinese came into the war in late November 1950 amounted to little more than pay records. I was to sort out not only my records, but also, as much as possible, those of the men that from my battalion aid station who had been lost, either killed or captured, when the Chinese forced us into the disastrous retreat from Kunu-ri.

I was also assigned other responsibilities on the trip. One was to supervise a dozen GIs who were being sent back to Division Rear for a variety of reasons, and another was to carry the regimental mail for posting. The latter duty was complicated by the fact that the Army Post Office in Miryang had burned to the ground two nights previously with, presumably, a great loss of mail, and I had no idea of where a replacement APO might have been set up. On the return trip I was to bring back four new second lieutenants being sent to us as replacements for line outfits, as well as supervising a truck load of 140 cases of whisky that constituted the long-awaited regimental whisky ration.

Miryang was where we had first bivouacked after arriving in South Korea from Japan in July, 1950. I was one of a planeload of young doctors, just out of their internships, who had been hurriedly called up to active duty and flown from the States to Japan.

We stayed a few days at an army hospital in Osaka while we were equipped with combat gear. We were also issued .45 caliber Colt-Browning automatic pistols and instructed in how to handle them. They were, of course, standard issue for officers.

We had then traveled by train down to Sasebo on the southernmost of the Japanese home islands. By ferry, we then made the overnight trip across the Sea of Japan to Pusan, the only major port still open in South Korea. We disembarked on the afternoon of 31 July 1950 into the stiflingly humid heat of the Korean summer and then traveled north by rail to Miryang on flatcars that were also carrying army trucks. It was located in the midst of the Pusan Perimeter area in the southeast corner of South Korea, the only part of the country that had not been conquered by the invading North Korean army.

Our trip south from the collecting station to Miryang by way of Chungju was essentially uneventful. There had been reports of roadblocks by guerillas lurking in the surrounding hills along the road, but we didn't run into any.

We stopped overnight of the first day with our regiment's Service Company that was still bivouacked near Yongju. It was even noisier at night there than at our collecting station, since the GIs pulling outpost sentry duty up on the hills surrounding this bivouac area were constantly banging away in the dark at what they thought might be enemy guerillas sneaking up on them. For all we knew, perhaps they really were scaring them away.

The road became much narrower and icy further south as it wound through higher snow-covered and increasingly mountainous terrain. This area was also thought to be infested with communist guerilla bands. After reaching much flatter country, we passed through the city of Taegu in what had been the northeast corner of the old Pusan

Perimeter. One of the largest cities in South Korea, it was now teeming with rear echelon US military units.

We arrived that afternoon in Miryang, 50 kilometers further to the south. The area seemed relatively untouched by the war. Many rear echelon Army support units were bivouacked near by. It was also noticeably warmer than it had been further north. Little else seemed changed since I had first seen the area seven months previously. With only a few traces of snow, it remained a rather pretty little South Korean town that was set in a valley near the eastern extension of the slow-flowing Naktong River.

After we found Division Rear, and delivered the twelve enlisted men to Division Personnel, we also found out where the new APO was located. I sent our truck driver, Cpl. Gonzales, to take the mail to it while I went to work in Personnel sorting out records. It didn't take anywhere near as long as I had expected. Put quite simply, considering how chaotic things were during our harrowing retreat from Kunu-ri, we didn't really know much about the fates of our personnel who were missing, and whether they had been killed or captured. It almost seemed as if they had simply been swallowed up in the massive chaos that had so disrupted the American forces after the Chinese army suddenly jumped into the war.

We learned that, to the north, our troops, their numbers now beginning to be bolstered by military forces being sent in from other countries that were members of the new United Nations, were again, if cautiously, beginning an offensive against the Chinese forces. However, things were still pretty well stalled in our division's sector south of Wonju.

A new general had arrived to take command of the division. He announced in no uncertain terms that many of our units were badly in need of better training, which didn't come as much of a surprise, and programs to accomplish this were to be instituted immediately, along with more intensive patrolling. There wasn't much time, with the enemy again massing to the north. Not unexpectedly, one of the first orders he issued was for all of us to shave off our whiskers.

Staying the night in the rather comfortable quarters provided by Division Rear was a real pleasure. I was again reminded of the fact that a soldier's lot in wartime was progressively better the further to the rear of the front lines he was stationed. If any of us had the choice, we would have much preferred an assignment as far as possible to the rear even though there would be no combat pay nor combat medic badges awarded back beyond regimental level.

The next morning, it took awhile to load the truck with the 140 cases of whisky. I wondered at the time whether we might be overloading the aging 2 1/2 ton vehicle. We then had to wait for the four new 2nd lieutenants to show up from the replacement depot a few miles away.

The lieutenants with their gear finally arrived in the early afternoon. Since I was the ranking officer, I again chose to ride in the cab with the driver, and the young lieutenants were to ride in the back of the truck, which was covered by an all-enclosing covered wagon type canvas tarp. Their initial ill-concealed displeasure with the arrangement soon dissolved into something like joy when they discovered what the truck was carrying.

There was a lot of military traffic on the road heading north that afternoon, and progress was slow. The road, still icy where it was in the shade, was often too narrow for us to pass slower truck convoys.

One convoy we did manage to pass was composed of four relatively slow-moving British Bedford lorries, or trucks, carrying UK troops. As we started to pass the last truck, one of the lieutenants, who had worked his way to the front of our truck bed, partially loosened the canvas tarp and tossed an opened whisky bottle into the back of the similarly-hooded British truck. Cpl. Gonzales, seeing what was happening, slowed down a little as we came alongside. As the back of our truck came level with the round opening in the top of the Bedford truck's cab that could be used for mounting a machine gun, one of the British soldiers stood up in it and pitched the now-empty bottle to the lieutenants in the back of our truck. This same process went on as we passed the other three trucks. It didn't look like a single drop of whisky was spilled. The whole process was facilitated by the British trucks being right hand drive, and having those circular openings in the cab tops for mounting machine guns on their left side.

CHAPTER 11

When we finally got up to Taegu after our much belated start and in slow traffic, the short winter day was rapidly coming to a close. I decided that, in consideration of the primitive roads through the mountains to the north that were again ahead of us, we would be wise to stop for the night and try to get a much earlier start the next morning.

After we found our way to the building devoted to housing transient military personnel, we also found a makeshift sort of garage near it where we could park our truck overnight. Cpl. Gonzales elected to unroll his sleeping bag and sleep in the truck, in part to guard the cargo. The four new 2nd Lieutenants and I unrolled our sleeping bags on cots in a barren unheated room in the Korean building. The place must have been some sort of a factory before the Army took it over. While raging battles had been fought early in the war not far from Taegu in the northwest corner of the old Pusan Perimeter, it had never been involved much in the fighting, so some relatively undamaged buildings were available.

One of the lieutenants produced a bottle, and passed it around. It hadn't been ten minutes before he got into a heated argument with another of the young officers. Soon, they were both grabbing for their .45 automatic pistols and threatening to go out in the street and fight a duel. It took a little while, but I finally got them calmed down.

Success to Stalemate in South Korea

There was an 8th Army mess hall nearby where we had dinner. The new lieutenants, probably as the result of sampling the truck's cargo all day, soon hit the sack. I decided that I needed some fresh air, and went outside to walk around.

It was already dark, but there was a lot of activity, and every thing was well illuminated by lights everywhere. I noticed that several GIs were flocking into the building adjacent to the mess hall. As I got closer, I could see that they were going into a room set up to show a movie. I found a seat on a folding chair just as they started the projector. The picture turned out to be "Mr. 880," and was most enjoyable.

Afterwards, as I walked past the mess hall on my way back to our temporary quarters, I saw that they were serving a late night meal, undoubtedly for the benefit of men in the many outfits nearby that were working around the clock. I went in and had a snack before turning in.

We were just starting to roll up our sleeping bags after breakfast as we prepared to depart, when Cpl. Gonzales reported that one of the truck's rear tires must have had a slow leak because it was now almost flat. I asked him if he knew where an 8th Army motor pool outfit might be located so he could get it fixed. He replied that that he thought he had seen one a block or so away.

The four lieutenants and I finished rolling up our sleeping bags and loaded them on the truck. Since the truck had four double tired rear wheels, it could still be readily driven to the motor pool for a replacement tire. Out of the corner of my eye I noticed that two of the lieutenants had been surreptitiously slipping bottles under their field jackets. I decided to make nothing of it, since we would now have another delay before getting started on our journey north.

We had time to walk around town a bit. Every building seemed to house one military outfit or another. There were a lot of tents, so the area had changed a great deal from what it had been like earlier in the war. There was a lot of not only foot but also vehicular traffic on the city's narrow streets. Interestingly enough, many of the vehicles belonged to military units coming into South Korea from other countries. They were, of course, drawn together by the commonly perceived need to stop the threat of communism spreading throughout south east Asia.

The nattiest of all the soldiers appeared to be those from the countries in the British Commonwealth. They were almost in stark contrast to the often rather scruffy appearance of our GIs in their multi-layered winter uniforms.

It was almost 1230 before Gonzales returned with the truck, having had a new tire and tube fitted. He reassured me that he had guarded it carefully. Because of the short winter day, we decided we would rather get on the road and have C-rations for lunch rather than take the time to go to the local mess.

Getting out of Taegu initially presented no problem but as we climbed into the hills to the north, the traffic became heavier and often slowed to a crawl. It seemed to me that there were fewer patches of ice than we had seen on the way down. Every once in a while, the traffic of trucks and jeeps would completely stop, usually because a vehicle ahead had partially slid off the road and had to be winched back up. It was a lot slower heading north out of town than it had been coming south.

We had only gone about 80 km, or 50 miles, when we neared the tiny town of Andong as winter darkness began to fall. We knew that our regimental tank company was bivouacked just south of the town, stalled there because the wintry roads so far hadn't permitted them to drive their massive M-4 Sherman tanks any further north.

Their outfit was relatively easy to find, since they needed a large and relatively flat area to park their tanks, not to mention all of their support vehicles. Such areas were few and far between, and the first such area off the side of the road proved to be the place. The tankers were most hospitable, perhaps because of the load our truck was carrying, and we soon had places for us to stay for the night in their warm tents.

Just before supper, the tankers got a call about taking one of their tanks to see if they could retrieve a truck that had gone off the road and into a ditch a mile or so away. I got to ride along, and learned that the huge Ford V-8 engines in the rear of the tanks, while producing something like 500 horsepower, would only get two miles out of every three gallons of fuel.

The road had become virtually empty of traffic as darkness began to fall. We soon found the truck. There was still enough light to see that it had turned over as it went off the road, spilling it's cargo over a wide area, and had landed upside down in a deep ditch. The driver had probably died from being pinned across his abdomen by the trucks' forward bulkhead as it tipped over. He had lost his helmet, but his unbroken glasses were still in position on his nose.

As it became even darker, it was decided that the truck could not be retrieved by the tank alone, and attempts to do so would best be left to a tank retriever in daylight the next morning. There was, of course, nothing we could do for the driver. Barely mentioned was concern about the possible threat presented by marauding guerilla bands that were said to be roaming the nearby hills, most notably after dark. When we got back to the tankers' bivouac area, the first shift of GIs acting as perimeter sentries were already being posted in their foxholes up on the surrounding low hills.

We learned that our regimental service company, bivouacked with all of its vehicles up the road in Yongju, and where we had stayed the first night on the way south, was planning to move north in two days. The tankers had also decided that with the road conditions improving, they would also try to move north at the same time. Considering that we still had to cross two more rather high passes through the mountains ahead of us, with the possibility of deteriorating weather, I decided that we would be well advised to spend the next night again with our service company so we could move out the following morning with it and the tanks.

John Benton

Then, it occurred to me that that there might be some medical school friends of mine in some of the units bivouacked near Yongju. This included an infantry regiment assigned to clearing out guerillas, and the medical clearing station of another division. I hoped to have ample time to make a few phone calls and see if we all might be able to get together that next evening. Considering what our truck was carrying, it could turn out to be a rather good party.

CHAPTER 12

We arrived back at Collecting in the early afternoon of the 21st. It was still located near a little village called Sindae-ni, just outside of Chupo-ri.

While preparing to leave the service company's bivouac area near Yongju earlier that morning, we learned that during the previous night all but two of the GIs on perimeter sentry duty in the hills around the service company's bivouac area had been charged with deserting their posts.

I had to laugh, if a bit ruefully. Not only had a few of my friends shown up, the fact that there was going to be a party attracted several officers from units of the infantry division and the nearby medical clearing station. They had all gathered together in one of the service company's squad tents the previous evening. The idea of a truck passing through that was loaded with whisky proved to be very appealing.

All of the officers didn't come empty handed, some bringing bottles of their own, and I contributed a few more from the truck. However, it wasn't long before one of the clearing station doctors announced that they had just gotten in a new and generous supply of medical alcohol, which was, of course, about 190 proof, and went off to get some of it. Then, one of our regiment's supply officers jumped up as he announced that they had a great supply of canned grapefruit juice. The result was that the party really took off, and the singing began in earnest. As it turned out, we used up very little of our load of whisky.

All of us who had participated in the affair instantly, and sheepishly, understood what had happened to those sentries. The poor scared, half-frozen and miserable GIs pulling duty out in those scattered foxholes on the high ground around the area somehow managed to misinterpret the incoherent sounds of our singing, tossed about as it was by a fitful 20 degrees or more below zero wind, as the legendary shouts of attacking Chinese. The next morning, the service company, quite understandably, hurried up the final loading of their trucks so that they could escape from the area as quickly as possible.

The last segment of our trip was relatively easy. We traveled along behind the service company's vehicles that in turn were following the tanks and their many support vehicles. When we arrived back into the vicinity of the Chupo-ri area, the tanks and the service company peeled off to their assigned bivouac areas near regimental headquarters. I had Cpl. Gonzales drop me off at Collecting before he drove over to the regimental motor pool area, where the truck would be unloaded, and the four lieutenants would report in for duty at regimental headquarters.

Bill Sloan and Bob Howard were standing in front of our receiving tent. I got a good grip on my sleeping bag, hung the sling of my carbine over my shoulder, and as I stepped down from the trucks cabs and said, "It looks like things are pretty slow around here."

"For once, they are," Sloan replied. "Welcome back. We thought you got lost and spirited away by the gooks."

"Road problems," I replied, "and some tire trouble. Why is it so quiet?"

Howard shook his head. "All of our battalions are out just patrolling roads from here up to Wonju and around it. They don't seem to be running into much. All we've been getting in has been the usual sick call stuff."

Sloan lit a cigarette. "How are things with the rear echelon heroes?"

"Warmer, for one thing," I replied. "They like to bitch about not getting the same kind of whisky rations that the line outfits do."

"Tough shit," said Howard. "My ass bleeds for them. You really did get all that booze up here okay?"

I nodded, although the proper answer might have been something on the order of most of it. "We were pretty careful."

Sloan wrinkled his forehead. "Don't you have to account for all of it?"

"They give us a ten percent overage in case of any breakage," replied Howard. "If you're careful, nobody gets short changed."

"Now I know why I'm glad he's back," Sloan said.

"Watch out for the chaplains," Howard replied. "Remember that they have an absolutely unerring instinct about where and when a bottle is being opened."

"Well," Sloan replied, "since we haven't been having any bottles to open for quite a while, it may be why we haven't seen much of them lately."

I only had time to get my sleeping bag unrolled on my cot in the blackout tent that I shared with Sloan before a few of Collecting's officers began to troop in. Canteen cups were produced as I somewhat reluctantly opened a bottle of Old Angus Scotch whisky. I poured what I guessed was somewhere between one and two ounces into each proffered cup. The ritual was to then add a little water from one's canteen.

Howard lifted his canteen cup, and said, "Here's to hyakuing the hell out of Korea."

We all murmured, "Here, here."

"I bet I know something that you bastards don't," said Sloan, as he wiped his lips with the back of his hand.

"And what in the hell might that be?" I asked.

Sloan smiled. "I just heard that Army really is setting up a rotation plan for medical officers."

"Where the hell did you hear that?" I took another sip. "I didn't hear a damned thing about it down at Division Rear, although there was a rumor going around here a few days ago about an R & R plan."

"No, this is different," Sloan replied. "I heard about it this morning when I was talking to a guy in the Division Surgeon's office. He said they had just gotten a memo about a program being planned for rotating medical officers from Korea back to hospitals in Japan. The guys are supposed to be rotated by the dates of when they first got here."

"Jesus," I said, "it's sure something to drink to, if it's for real."

"When is all this supposed to happen?" Howard asked.

"Pretty damned soon," Sloan replied. "I doubt if it will apply to me, since I'm on Temporary Duty."

I again poured drinks for the others, as Howard asked, "Did they say anything about us MSC guys?"

"He never mentioned it," Sloan said, "but it would certainly make sense. A lot of you people got here before most of the medical officers."

"I'll for damned sure be getting on the horn to Division first thing in the morning to check it out," Howard replied.

I thought to look at my watch, and announced, "If we're going to get to the chow line before the cooks close it down, we better get our asses in gear."

As I stuffed the partially emptied bottle into the barracks bag under my cot, I thought that, just maybe, there would now be something to look forward to, after all. However, I had to remember that since our division had not been the first to arrive in South Korea, it could obviously take a while before any such program would get around to us.

I also noted that no one had said a word about the sacking of the Division's commanding general.

CHAPTER 13

Collecting had been bivouacked in one place long enough for us to begin to settle in. We had even managed to find a radio that could pick up programs from an armed forces station in Japan that provided popular Stateside music and news broadcasts.

Because of the typically rough, unpaved, and often iced-up South Korean roads, often iced-up, and the snow, the litter jeeps couldn't travel much faster than fifteen or twenty miles per hour on the way in from the battalion aid stations. As a result, we often were busy until well past midnight. It also meant serious delays in getting the wounded to Clearing Stations.

Since, for the time being, our regiment's line companies weren't running into much enemy activity, most of the GIs we were seeing on sick call were from attached units that were bivouacked near us. One was a combat engineer company that was improving a nearby airstrip. It seemed almost as if the majority of their people, from the company commander on down, were on our sick call nearly every day. There were also GIs from an anti-aircraft outfit that was being used as mobile light artillery in support of ground troops, the regimental tank company, and a nearby field artillery battalion.

We were still seeing what we were pretty sure were self-inflicted wounds nearly every day. Of course, we couldn't report such things without having at least some proof. However, GIs continued to be loath to "rat" on their buddies.

Then, I had to fill in for the medical officer in one of our battalion stations that was bivouacked in Sillim-ni, a tiny village about halfway between Chechon and Wonju. The medical officer had to go down to Taegu for what we thought would be just a day or two at the most. This left all the medical care at Collecting to Bill Sloan.

The battalion I was visiting, like our regiment's other two battalions, was still mostly engaged in patrolling roads for signs of the enemy without encountering much. A motorized patrol was able to penetrate northward all the way to the southern outskirts of Hoensong without meeting enemy resistance. While we appreciated the respite, we were all too aware that the CCF and the NKPA were still up there somewhere and undoubtedly marshalling their considerable forces for another massive attack in the not-too-distant future.

The battalion aid station had taken over what appeared to be, at least for South Korea, a middle-class dwelling, and the aid men were living more comfortably than would be the case in the usual battalion aid station setup. They had their blackout tent erected near the door of the house.

I hardly had the chance to drop my gear before the aid station's chief medic came in with a medical tag in his hand and a look of desperation on his face.

"I hate to bother you, sir," he said, "seeing as how you just got here, but I got a guy here who's been giving us real problems."

"Another goldbrick?"

The sergeant shook his head. "No, I think maybe he could be plain crazy. His company CO, Capt. Walters, just sent him down here with one of our medics who's out with his company. He told the medic to tell us that he wanted this guy evacuated for damned sure this time."

"That sounds pretty ominous," I said, as I started to load my pipe. "What in hell has he done?"

The sergeant shook his head. "Aw, the guys say he's a chronic fuck-up. He's a replacement that came in just before we moved back from Wonju. A week ago he was in here complaining about a bellyache, and we evacuated him back to Collecting thinking he might have appendicitis."

As I lit my pipe, I realized that I didn't remember any case like that coming through Collecting, and then thought that probably Sloan had processed him while I was on my trip down to Miryang. I asked, "How long was he gone?"

"Just a few days. They apparently didn't operate on him or anything."

"It should have been long enough," I replied, "for somebody to figure out whether he was a psycho or just a goldbrick."

Lt. Bill Armstrong, the MSC officer with the aid station, ducked under the low lintel of the native house as he pushed the covering blanket aside, and said, "Hi, Captain. Nice to have you here. Sergeant Miles, don't tell me you were talking about Ollie Winters from Item Company? Those rear-echelon bastards couldn't have sent him back to us again so soon!"

"They sure did, Lieutenant," the sergeant replied.

"Jesus H. Christ," said Armstrong, as he lit a cigarette. "I bet that really pissed off Walters."

I shook my head. "Hey, what's with this guy?"

Armstrong exhaled smoke. "He's the worst misfit I've ever seen. He's a scrawny little bastard and a real eight-ball that can't seem to get anything right. One night he threw a hand grenade box that still contained a couple of them in it to feed a fire. He was as lucky as shit to get away with it, and not hurt anyone else either. He's also always bothering the company medics for pills."

"My kid brother would like to strangle him," said the sergeant.

"Your brother?" I said.

"Yeah, when he got drafted and sent over here, he asked to be in the same outfit with me. He's one of the medical corpsman out with this guys's company."

"His brother's a damned good aid man," Armstrong said.

I frowned. "What's the guy complaining about now?"

"He says he has tuberculosis," the sergeant replied.

"What seems to make him think that?" I picked up a field medical tag.

"Maybe," Armstrong said, "he came up with the idea because he's figured it out that we'd have to evacuate him for a chest x-ray to be sure."

"Sounds like he may be crazy like a fox," I replied.

"Could be," said Armstrong. "I wouldn't surprised if all the dumb stuff he pulls off is just part of a big act to get his ass out of here for good. We've got too many more like him, but none of them anywhere near as bad as he is."

"But," I said, "it's interesting that his company commander sure doesn't seem to want him back."

"You can sure say that again, Captain," said the sergeant. "He's just too damned weird. Having him around could be really bad for morale."

I shook my head, and said, "Morale seems to be bad enough around here as it is. I guess I better go over to the tent and take a look at him."

"Happy to lead the way," said Armstrong. "Follow me."

He pulled back the blanket taking the place of a door and again ducked under the low door. The sergeant and I followed. The tent was only a few steps away.

As I squeezed my way through the black-out flaps, I could see that there were two GIs in the tent. One, standing, had a field medical aid kit hanging from his right shoulder and an M2 carbine hanging on a sling over the left. I realized that he must be the younger brother of Sgt. Miles, who had followed me into the tent. Almost all of the combat medics out with the line companies had been carrying weapons since early in the war. It was no secret that there had already been countless occasions when they actually had to use them.

The other was a slightly built man with rather disheveled clothing, hardly out of his teens, who was sitting on the dirt floor near a gasoline-fired heater. He was not carrying a weapon, and was wearing a soft cap normally worn under a steel helmet but without the helmet. He also had at least two day's worth of beard, and I thought he had something

Success to Stalemate in South Korea

of the look of a ferret. He would cough every minute or so while holding a fist over his mouth while his eyes darted towards me.

I realized that I hadn't heard him coughing until he could see me coming into the tent. As I picked up a stethoscope that was lying on a medical tray, I told him to stand up and pull up his shirt so I could listen to his chest. This process involved pulling up a long john underwear shirt, a wool shirt, a sweater, a cotton twill shirt-jacket, and a field jacket.

As I listened, while positioning the bell of the stethoscope over various areas of his back, I noted that he was clever enough to tighten up his throat when he breathed, producing rather raspy breath sounds. I tricked him by asking him questions, which meant he had to relax his throat to answer, and which, of course, stopped the rasping. I could see that he was watching me out of the corner of his eye. Whatever else he might have been, he was clearly not completely stupid.

"I'm pretty bad off, huh, Doc?"

"Hard to say," I replied slowly, as I folded the stethoscope and put it down. "How long have you had the cough?"

He coughed loudly, "Maybe three days, Sir."

"Are you spitting up anything?"

"Uh, maybe a little snot. I wheeze a lot when I can't catch my breath."

I told the man to get his clothes straightened out and wrote down the GI's complaints on the tag, noting that his temperature was normal, and that his lungs were clear to auscultation with breath sounds that were normal when he wasn't trying to make them otherwise. While I was sure his complaints were spurious, there seemed to be deeper problems. Yet, I felt uncomfortable as well as uncertain about trying to make a psychiatric diagnosis, having had so little training in how to deal with psychosomatic disorders.

He was, somehow, very different from the usual run of malingerers that we had been seeing. Maybe, I thought, if they would work him up properly somewhere in the rear, medical officers with more experience than I did would be better able to sort out his problem. I also couldn't forget that the sheer presence of this guy had become a real problem with the other members of his unit. There also didn't seem to be any point to holding him at Collecting for a few days to see if he would shape up. There seemed to be much more wrong with him than just combat fatigue. On his field medical tag I quickly wrote, "Evac. for chest x-ray and pulm. consult, may have psych. problems."

Handing the tag back to Miles, I said, "Send him on down to Collecting, Sergeant. Make sure that the Major sees his field tag. This guy may be a real head case, but I kind of hate to write things like that on the tag."

Sgt. Miles nodded, then turned to his brother and said, "You heard the man. Wake up one of the jeep drivers, and be sure to tell him to pick up a few jerry cans full of gas on the way back."

The medic signaled to the GI who was, I thought, perhaps doing his best to conceal a smile, and hustled him out of the tent.

"If my kid brother has to be here," said Miles, "I'm sure glad it's with us."

"Sounds good to me." I replied. "I sure hope what I wrote on that tag will at least keep that guy away from here for awhile, and maybe he'll get lost in the shuffle or be sent somewhere else. He sure could be a real psycho case, and I hope they recognize it this time before trying to send him back."

Armstrong laughed. "Bob Walters will appreciate that. He's convinced that the guy is raving nuts, and that it's dangerous to have him around."

I shook my head. "Any GI in a line rifle outfit that comes in here under his own power, without a helmet and a weapon, has a good chance of being at least a malingerer until proven otherwise."

Armstrong nodded. "At least it will make Walters happy to get him the hell out of his company. Guys like him can be real bad apples in the barrel."

CHAPTER 14

Later that day, I learned a little more about the new rotation scheme to military hospitals in Japan. It apparently had suddenly stalled after only a few medical officers had been transferred because it was rather belatedly realized that only a very few medical officers were coming in as replacements. It was also suddenly realized that the contemplated program would have to wait until the Army medical officers who were classified as being on TDY, or temporary duty, and the many Navy medical officers, now serving with the Army, had all been replaced. Since, so far, we were still getting only a very few Army medical officer replacements, it was obviously doubtful when the program could be implemented.

We had a little excitement late in the afternoon when some men led in four scrawny cows they found wandering around. They had probably been left behind to shift for themselves by farmers who had long since fled south. With visions of steaks dancing in their heads, the GIs decided to sacrifice the largest one. For nearly half an hour, they chased the poor animal around while blazing away at it with carbines and automatic pistols before they finally dropped it. It was a wonder they didn't drop a few of each other.

The weather continued clear and bright, with midday temperatures a bit above freezing. Mangy birds, perhaps sparrows, appeared. While it continued to be quiet in our sector, we heard that a motorized patrol from another regiment had run into surprisingly stiff enemy resistance while probing north of Hoensong. It was believed that this confirmed the fact that the Chinese were indeed still very much in the area and undoubtedly completing preparations for a soon-to-be-launched major attack.

On the 26th of January, the battalion aid station moved up nearer to Wonju along with the battalion headquarters. Motorized patrols up to as far as the southern outskirts of Hoensong and to the east and west still reported failure to contact any enemy. The aid station had again found a rather comfortable Korean house. Indeed, my biggest problem seemed to be that I was running low on pipe tobacco.

We were still receiving few battle casualties, just sick call and non-combat injuries mostly from motor vehicle accidents. However, the battalion commander came by to see me that afternoon He had some respiratory complaints and clinical findings that all added up to possible pulmonary tuberculosis. Of course, I could not confirm it in the battalion aid station. I promptly had him packed off by jeep directly to a division clearing station in Chungju where they could do a proper work-up with x-rays and blood tests. As soon as he left, the S-5, a major, who would now be taking over command of the battalion, broke out a bottle of good Scotch.

After dealing with a few men on sick call that day with clear-cut scabies, I sat down to deal with my income tax status. I had been told that I would be issued a W-2 form for tax filing. I was having $65 a month docked for withholding tax. I then realized that I might as well forget about it since I would have six months after returning to the States, when and if that ever happened, to sort out my tax status.

On the 28th, the battalion aid station moved back to Sillim-ni. We were at last able to institute an ongoing program for test firing our weapons, another of the new procedures that had been mandated by General Ridgway soon after he had taken over command of Eighth Army. We were also now told to expect much maneuvering as the Army

Success to Stalemate in South Korea

units advanced and withdrew as part of a new approach to fighting the war. The plan was to emphasize decimating the enemy forces by killing as many of their soldiers as possible, rather than just quibbling over gaining or losing real estate. However, our objectives would undoubtedly still have us moving ever further north.

Shortly after we finished setting up the aid station, and while it was still light, a military police sergeant working with the headquarters company called me and told me they were bringing in a GI to get him checked out medically. They told me that he had been squatting in a pup tent with an M1 rifle across his knees out in Item Company's area, daring anyone to come near him. The rest of the infantry company was staying well clear of him and did not seem much interested in challenging the GI.

I learned that there actually were two MPs involved. While one of them tried to talk to the GI and in so doing focus his attention, the other had quietly slipped off to one side and worked his way around behind the little tent, and grabbed the GI from behind. When they brought him into the Aid Station's blackout tent, both having a good grip on him, I recognized that the unkempt GI was in fact Ollie Winters.

I wondered how in hell he could've gotten back so quickly. When I examined him, he was sullen and quite subdued, gave no indication of recognizing me, and I couldn't help but notice some welts and bruises over his upper body that looked rather fresh. I again sent him to the rear in short order with the two MPs, and in no uncertain terms demanded psychiatric evaluation in large letters on his Field Medical Tag. We thought that this time we would never see him again.

We even had what was at first called an air raid alert later that night. We thought we heard airplane engines, and we could see a few flares in the sky several miles away.

The North Koreans occasionally did fly what the GIs were wont to call "bedcheck charlies" at night over our lines. The aircraft usually were Russian Polikarpov two seater biplanes, really almost relics of the 1920s but sturdy, and used mostly for aerial observation. Later the next day Division informed us, rather apologetically, that what we heard had been our planes, after all.

When the battalion surgeon finally returned the next day, I returned to Collecting, still bivouacked near Chupo-ri. It continued to be a bit warmer, perhaps heralding the anticipated breaking up of the winter weather sometime during the next month or so.

The number of men getting "Dear John" letters was becoming something of a problem. This mainly involved the men who had been in Korea for the longest time. Wives seemed to be deciding to get a divorce rather than waiting any longer for them to return. It certainly wasn't good for morale, and counseling these men kept our three regimental chaplains very busy.

While our sector was still relatively quiet, we heard that a patrol from a regiment to the west of us, while checking out a narrow little valley called the "twin tunnels" area, had gotten into trouble. The area was so named because the rather narrow valley was crossed by a railroad track that ran through tunnels in the steep hills on both sides. The GIs had been suddenly surrounded by what was thought to be at least two well-equipped North Korean battalions. The patrol was finally extricated with a great deal of difficulty.

When we learned that our regiment was soon to go into reserve somewhere in the rear near Chungju, we held a celebratory poker game in the collecting tent that night. I later figured out that I had lost a total of $2.07.

CHAPTER 15

Late in the afternoon on February 1st, while still in regimental reserve, the collecting station moved up to a position about 9 kilometers southwest of Wonju. Seemingly endless streams of refugees, looking ever more pathetic, were still moving grimly down roads to the south.

Early in the war, North Korean soldiers, then relentlessly driving back the fledgling ROK army and the ill-equipped and ill-trained American forces that had been rushed in to help them, would often hide amongst crowds of refugees fleeing to the south. Sometimes, they drove hapless refugee groups ahead of their units as human shields. The outnumbered, ill-trained and frightened GIs faced some very difficult decisions as they fired their machine guns in the attempt to slow the better-trained and equipped communist North Korean Peoples Army. Such situations made civilian casualties inevitable. I thought it was interesting that the Chinese didn't seem to use such tactics.

The road we took, recently and hurriedly put through by the engineers and intended to be a short cut to the Yoju-Wonju road, was just about the worst we had seen. It became little more than a quagmire as our vehicles churned up the muddy ground that, while frozen at night, thawed during the slightly warmer days. It wasn't until nearly midnight when we arrived at our chosen bivouac area near another tiny deserted farmers' village. As was so often the case, nobody seemed to know it's name, or even if it had a name.

The few reasonably intact native dwellings nearby looked as if they were being used as rest stops by the south-bound refugees. We decided to avoid them and just put up our tents on an adjacent flat area. Setting up our electric lighting was much facilitated by the fact that we had recently acquired a portable gasoline powered generator and no longer had to rely on electricity supplied by auto batteries. Having to rotate them in and out of vehicles so that they were kept charged up enough to keep our electric lights working had been a real nuisance. However, we still had use for the gasoline fired lanterns.

As soon as we had our tents erected, three casualties were brought in. One, picked up along the way by one of our ambulances, was a young GI complaining of a leg being injured when a loaded ammo box fell on it while he was loading supplies on a truck. Since he had dozed off while lying on one of the litters in the ambulance and I had to awaken him to find out what his problem was, I knew that he wasn't too badly hurt. Another was one of our jeep drivers complaining of a stomach ache, but after an essentially negative examination, I treated him with soda bicarb and amytal pills and decided to hold him overnight. When he showed up for breakfast the next morning I recognized that he was probably doing okay.

The third patient was all too familiar. I could hardly believe it. It was none other than Ollie Winters, yet again. I well remembered the times that I had him evacuated and asked for psychiatric evaluation, the last time just a few days previously. Even so, here he was again. His battalion surgeon probably didn't know what else to do with him except to send him back to us. I could hardly believe that any medical officer in a rear echelon medical unit, and who was in his right mind, could have sent a man with Ollie's history back to duty in a combat infantry outfit without first ordering the psychiatric evaluation that we had so urgently requested.

When I started to examine him while he sat on a litter supported by a medical storage chest at each end that we used for an examining table, he seemed quieter than he had been on previous occasions. I was just starting to ask him about his complaints when Sgt. Henderson called me to one side. He then handed me a hand-written note from the commander of Ollie's line company. The driver of the litter jeep that brought him in from the battalion aid station had been ordered to give it to "the collecting station Med. Officer." I noted that the battalion aid station medical officer had noted on the Field Medical Tag attached to Ollie's field jacket, "Urgent Psych. Evaluation."

In the note, the GI's company commander had written that this time he wanted Ollie evacuated as a serious nut case. He demanded that he be sent back for a real psychiatric evaluation, and "...not just be promptly bounced back to duty by some iron-assed rear echelon quack medical officer who only briefly listens to his weird complaints without going any deeper into his problems." He further wrote that Ollie, back from his last evacuation for only a day, had been loudly insisting that he be reassigned as a cook, rather than a rifleman. He further noted that if he ever found Ollie in his outfit's mess kitchen he would seriously consider drowning him in the coffee vat. We certainly needed men, but not ones like Ollie.

I thanked the sergeant. Then, I asked, "I'm sure you remember seeing this guy come through here before."

"Hell, yes, Captain," Henderson replied. "He's a real eight-ball."

I nodded, and turned back to Ollie. "What's your problem this time, soldier?"

Ollie, as on the other occasions when I had seen him, was a mess. He said, slowly, "I think the Captain really thinks I'm crazy."

"Oh?" I replied, trying not to sound too sarcastic.

"Well, I ain't crazy. I jus' don' wanna be no goddamned rifleman."

That was interesting, no weird complaints, just maybe something that was reasonably close to the truth.

"Nobody really wants to be," I replied.

"I don't wanna get my ass shot off in this stupid war while I'm just standing there holding a fuckin' M-1 rifle."

I realized that few of us could argue that point. Maybe he really wasn't all that crazy after all.

I said, "Think of your buddies in the squad."

"Fuck 'em," he replied.7 "I got a sick mother with nobody much to help her. I gotta get out of here alive so I can take care of her."

Interesting, I thought. Maybe he hadn't heard of hardship discharges and the like for soldiers with bad family problems, or maybe he'd already been turned down since they weren't granted very often. If they weren't, just about every GI in the rifle companies might have been trying to get one. This time he didn't seem to have any physical complaints. He just wanted to get another assignment that was less dangerous, so he could survive to take care of his mother, or so he said. Maybe he wasn't really a psycho, or was he?

Again, I also added a request for a proper psychiatric evaluation on the man's field medical tag. I also attached the company CO's note to the tag, hoping that this time someone in Clearing would pay more attention and have the good sense to send him further back to the rear where he could get the requested evaluation. While we needed to keep all the men on the line that we could, we certainly didn't need any like Ollie.

It all made me reflect, as I so often did, on the fact that maybe we weren't there for just treating injuries and disease. Rather, we were to prevent men in line outfits from being evacuated by presenting dubious and likely spurious physical complaints. It was officially known as "maintaining combat capability."

Yet, there was always the concern that we might be wrong at times. Just because we couldn't seem to find anything wrong with men we dismissively called "goldbricks" was no guarantee that they didn't have perhaps serious problems that we were simply unable to detect. As the war progressed, we tended to give them more of a hard time than sympathy.

Success to Stalemate in South Korea

It must also be noted that our collecting station had already acquired the reputation of the having one of the lowest non-battle casualty evacuation rates. Maybe we had already become a bit too hard-nosed.

Charley Morse came back later that day from one of his trips to division supply with a rather disturbing story. He said that he had heard that it involved some of the personnel of the collecting station of an infantry regiment over to the west that was bivouacked near one of the main north-south roads. It was apparently near a little native village, apparently much like the one near us, that was also being used as a rest stop by refugees fleeing south.

It seems, so the story went, that two or three of the medics in that outfit had noticed a rather attractive girl in one group of refugees that was stopping over in the village. So, they went back to the collecting station and got a lot of capsules of sodium amytal, a barbiturate drug that was often used as a sedative. After emptying one capsule, they went into back the native house with one of their KATUSAs as an interpreter and passed out the capsules to the adults of the group, and gave the empty capsule to the girl. They had apparently told the poor Koreans that it was medicine to prevent cholera, known to be running rampant among the refugees.

After an hour or so, they apparently went back to find all the refugees in the room sound asleep just as they had expected, except, of course, the girl. Then, so the story went, they carefully moved her away from the others and took turns raping her.

The next morning, they returned, to find that all of the refugees were dead, including the girl. Exactly why they should all be dead was not included in the story as told, which made it very difficult to take for granted.

I never heard anything more about the incident, bizarre and not very credible as it was. Such things, in isolated settings, with no witnesses, or perhaps none willing to come forth, could well have happened, only to easily soon become overshadowed and forgotten in the midst of an ongoing vicious war. While it might well have been just another example of the wild, fanciful, and quite improbable, to say the least, rumors that were constantly being circulated, I have often wondered if such a thing might have actually happened.

The American units and their United Nations allies cautiously probing north of Wonju soon found themselves engaging in shifting and sporadic fighting. The "Twin Tunnels" area continued to be a problem. As the result, we hadn't been able to send a Dutch soldier, who had come in on sick call two days previously with diarrhea and had since recovered, back to his unit that was engaged there.

CHAPTER 16

The next day, we learned that a Corps shower unit with heated tents had been set up on the bank of a river less than a quarter of a mile from our bivouac area. Several of us promptly visited it, since it had been months since we had been able to take a decent bath. Also, another regimental whisky ration came in late in the afternoon. I had ordered three bottles, one each of MacNaughton's Scotch, Schenley's V.O., and Canadian Club.

After dinner, when things were almost unusually quiet, one of the sergeants wanted to talk to me privately. Many of Collecting's officers were off on business of one sort or another. Major Sloan was over at Regiment for an Officers' Call meeting. We sat down in one end of the deserted main squad tent. The man was a very able NCO, and, indeed, I thought worthy of even being considered for a battlefield MSC commission. It turned out that he was having marital troubles like so many others of our GIs.

After a few minutes, when I had just lighted my pipe, we heard what sounded to me like a round fired from a .45 automatic. The sergeant stopped in mid-sentence, and then said. "Did you hear that, Captain?"

I looked around. "I sure did. It sounded like a .45."

"It was also pretty close to us here."

I looked at the sergeant for a brief moment. Then, I jumped up, knocked out my pipe, and said, "Let's go!"

After picking up a flashlight, I ducked my head as I went out through the tent flaps, to pause as I wondered for a moment about where the shot had been fired

The sergeant, right behind me, said, "Sir, I think it might have come from over by the officers' tent."

I nodded. Everything was very quiet. Regrettable as it was, it was not all that unusual to hear a shot or two fired in our area just after the whisky rations came in, but little damage was usually done, the miscreants usually being put to bed and sometimes "busted down" in rank the next day. Still, I was concerned because this shot seemed so close. We already had seen one GI who had been inadvertently shot in the leg by a buddy who was supposed to be cleaning his rifle. Mercifully, it had been an uncomplicated wound.

It wasn't far to the officers' quarters tent, marked by bits of yellow light trickling out around the closed flaps covering it's entrance. I realized that the new snow was effectively muffling our footsteps.

The sergeant, following me, whispered in my ear, saying, "Sir, I've got the feeling that something real funny's going on."

I nodded in the dark, realizing that I shared his concern, as I switched off the flashlight and shoved it into a pocket as we neared the tent entrance. When we reached the flaps, I swept them aside, and stepped into the tent.

"Okay, off your asses and on your feet, you've got visitors," I announced, in what I hoped was a reasonably jocular way.

I was ill prepared for what I immediately saw in the flickering yellow light of a gasoline lantern hanging on the central tent pole. The Motor Pool officer, Ed Jones, was sitting on a cot near the tent entrance with a .45 automatic in his hand and an empty whisky bottle at his feet. Across from him and sitting on cots were the two dentists who looked very frightened, and Bob Howard. Jones looked more than drunk, and was brandishing the .45 around, sometimes pointing it at his own head and sometimes at the other men. I had no doubt that the piece had a round in the chamber with the safety off. He was speaking almost incoherently and did not seem to recognize that I was standing there.

Suddenly racing through my mind was remembering that the man had gotten rather drunk a couple of times previously after whisky rations came in, although he had behaved well enough. He certainly had always seemed to me to be a pleasant enough guy and a good officer.

While it was never too obvious, I had gotten the strong impression that he and Howard had long been very much at odds with each other, perhaps because of something that had happened between them in the distant past. I did know that Jones had become convinced he was being passed over for promotion, and had decided that it was all Howard's fault. I also knew that he was also unhappy with what he suspected his wife might be doing back in the States. All that, plus the whisky, may have suddenly tipped him over the edge. I couldn't tell whether he was seriously intent on shooting Bob, to kill himself, or perhaps both. He had already fired at least the one round, although it looked like he had missed hitting anyone, or, even, anything, except for putting another hole in the tent.

"What the hell do you think you're doing, Lieutenant," I shouted. "Put that goddamned piece down now!"

Jones shook his head, as if trying to clear it, as he turned towards me. The words so slurred that they were almost unintelligible, he said, "That you, Doc?"

"You're goddamned right it's me." I wondered what in hell I could do to sort out this crazy situation. "Don't you think you better go hit the sack?"

He slowly shook his head "No fucking sack for me until I take care of this mother-fucking asshole."

Then, I had an idea. I realized that the sergeant, perhaps wisely, had not come all the way into the tent, having stopped just at the entrance behind me, but he certainly had to have seen what was going on. I tried to signal him behind my back with my right hand, since Jones' view of the tent entrance was blocked by my body, to come up closer behind me.

I said, "Howard's not doing a damned thing to you. He's just sitting there. What about Ramirez and Weill?"

Jones started to slide off the end of the cot, but clumsily pulled himself back up with one hand while he pointed the gun again at Howard.

He slurred, "I'm not mad at them, except they're asshole Howard's buddies."

Then, he took off on a long rambling sort of speech with words falling over each other about how Howard, as his commanding officer, was ruining his career in the Army, while he continued to aimlessly wave the gun around. It was all too apparent that he had already gotten himself into very deep trouble, and I almost prayed that I could somehow find a way bring this crazy situation to a conclusion without someone getting hurt, or worse.

Turning to me, Jones said, 'Do you know this bastard is trying to screw me?"

"Come on, Ed," I replied. "Who gives a damn? Why don't you just go hit the sack and you can tell me about it in the morning. You know I'm your friend."

"That's for fucking-A right, Doc, you're one of the damned few I have around here!" Jones fished a khaki-colored handkerchief out of a pocket with his left hand and blew his nose, while managing to keep the .45 pointed at Howard.

I sensed that the sergeant had come up close behind me. Turning my head only slightly, I said as quietly as I could, "pentothal in a syringe now!"

The faint rustle of the sergeant's clothing reassured me that he had gotten the message and was on the way. Jones was beginning to look like he was getting sleepy. The two dentists had hardly moved. Howard looked like he was planning how to jump and try to disarm Jones as soon as he thought there would be a chance of succeeding. I wasn't so sure that it would be a good idea, since attempting such a move could go very wrong.

As casually as I could, I said, "Would you mind telling me what the fuck is going on here?" I tried to laugh a little as I added, "Nobody ever tells me shit about these things."

Jones turned towards me. "Christ, I don't think there's much..." He swung back, alert again, as Howard started to rise as if he was about to make his move. "Get your miserable son-of-a-bitchin' ass back down on that cot or I'll blow your cock-sucking head off!"

Howard sat down slowly, saying nothing, but I noticed that he was almost hyper alert. The situation, dangerous as it had been, was getting worse. Trying to sound calm, I realized that I had to keep Jones talking, as I fervently wished for the sergeant's quick return.

"Like I was saying, Ed, clue me in about what this is all about."

After a moment, Jones replied, clearly enough, "Doc, you would never believe the rations of shit this motherfucker has been handing me. Every time he sends in my personnel evaluation report, he shits all over me. I've had it with the son-of-a bitch. I'm gonna square things right now and I hope he burns in hell."

Jones was raising the .45, as if taking careful aim. With a gush of relief, I heard a slight rustle of the curtains over the tent entrance flaps, and then felt a syringe being pressed into my hand that was outstretched behind me.

"You know, Ed," I said, trying to sound casual, "if you pull that trigger, your ass will sure be grass."

Without turning his head, Jones replied. "It don't make no mother fucking difference. I've got almost a full clip. There'll be a round left for me."

I wondered if Howard, from where he was sitting, could see what I had been doing with my right hand. I was almost sure he could. Maybe he was waiting for me to start something that he could help finish. Of course, the sergeant was also there behind me, and Jones certainly couldn't have seen him.

"Okay, okay, Ed," I said. "Would you mind if I sit down?"

"Makes me no difference," Jones replied. "Take your choice."

There weren't cots for me to sit on with out crossing in front of Jones, which I suddenly realized was an advantage.

As I started to move in front of him, I said, while pointing to a cot on the other side of him, "Ed, I hope you won't mind pointing that gun down while I go sit down over there."

"Christ, I'm not mad at you, Doc." He lowered the gun.

I very carefully walked in front of Jones, no knowing quite what to expect, while keeping my right hand out of his sight. When I was past him, I looked briefly at Howard, then turned as quickly as I could and jabbed the needle of the syringe through Jones' clothing and into his left upper arm, and quickly pushed down the plunger as hard as I could. Jones jerked around, clearly surprised, to look at me with suddenly wide opened eyes.

Howard was up on Jones in an instant, knocking the gun out of his hand. The sergeant was on Jones almost as fast, grabbing his right arm and twisting it around behind his back as he kicked the fallen .45 automatic under another cot.

As I withdrew the syringe, Jones started to say something incoherently. Then, he slumped back, quite unconscious. It could have been that it wasn't so much due to the quick-acting pentothal as it was to the whisky finally catching up with him. I realized that I could finally breath again.

We promptly sent the snoring Jones back to Clearing in an ambulance with two medics guarding him to make sure that if he awakened he wouldn't get loose. His future, overall not good at all, was uncertain, depending on whether he would be treated as a psycho, or court martialed for the attempted murder of an officer. We later learned that when the lieutenant arrived at the clearing station and after his medic guards explained the situation to the receiving medics, they promptly stationed a sergeant carrying a baseball bat to guard him.

CHAPTER 17

Two days later we were ordered to get ready to take part in an offensive operation named "Operation Roundup." The objective was to catch the enemy forces to the north off-balance while they were undoubtedly preparing for yet another major offensive and keep them that way, and in the process kill or capture as many of them as possible. While our regiment was still officially in reserve, our battalions, as part of their retraining, were being kept busy patrolling roads and setting up roadblocks behind the regiment's other outfits on the line that were beginning to be hit by enemy probing attacks.

That day I was busy with sick call all morning. It was a bit surprising to see how many GIs with questionable complaints were being sent to us from the battalion aid stations. The battalion medics still found it easier to get them out of their hair by shipping them off to us in Collecting, thus leaving it to us to make the final decisions about the merits of their professed problems.

I was involved with the emotional problems of men in Collecting in the afternoon. One of our gasoline-fired stoves exploded that evening, setting a little fire to the tent. Just as it was quickly extinguished by waving blankets, a litter jeep from one of the battalion aid stations brought in a GI that had a gunshot wound in the leg, sustained while he was loading a truck when another GI accidentally kicked a machine gun in a way that somehow caused it to fire.

The next day, "Roundup" jumped off. The freezing nights and warmer days continued to make a muddy mire of all our so-called roads that greatly impeded vehicular movement. A persistent overcast had prevented much aerial observation of the enemy for several days. Soon, the other two regiments of a division to the northwest became engaged in heavy fighting. Our regiment, positioned further to the east, was so far relatively untouched while our battalions that were patrolling area roads in support of nearby ROK units were sustaining only occasional wounded.

Meanwhile, mail and packages were coming in from the States much more regularly. We were even often having movies after dark when things were quiet. I was receiving periodic re-supplies from home of underwear that was much more comfortable than the GI issue. I was even beginning to get return letters from some of the condolence letters I had written months earlier to the families of men serving in my battalion aid station who had been killed. Some of the letters were pitiful almost beyond belief.

As it began to snow more often, sick call increased in numbers, not only from the battalions but also the regiment-level outfits. Unlike treating wounds, sprains, bone fractures, and the like, which was quite straightforward, trying to separate out the GIs that were really sick from the ones that were clever malingerers continued to be difficult.

We were able to keep pretty well informed about the increasingly ominous actions that were going on to the northwest of us, although it continued to be relatively quiet in our immediate area. We even learned that the name of the little village near where we were bivouacked was Lodol.

By the 9th of February, stubborn CCF pressure continued. As the weather started to clear, airdrops of supplies to forward-positioned troops were initiated since it was becoming too difficult to supply them by truck over the miserably muddy roads. When aerial observation could be resumed, large numbers of Chinese were seen massing north of Chipyong-ni, including one group with an estimated 1200 horses.

An estimated forty CCF became trapped in a mine near Wonju. The plan was to keep them hunkered down in it with artillery fire during the night, and in the morning, as they tried to escape, cut them down with machine gun fire as they emerged from the tunnels.

Two days later, as pressure from the CCF along the battle lines to the north west continued to increase despite all of our efforts to disrupt it, the unsuccessful Operation Roundup was called off. Our forces, now inclusive of ever more units from other countries who were coming in under the banner of the United Nations, were now ordered to try to break off contact with the enemy. We were to then pull back while a defense line was being organized around Wonju in preparation for the long-expected big enemy offensive, as well as to continue to send out strong combat patrols to monitor the enemy's progress. Some of the newer ROK divisions, admittedly ill-trained and ill-equipped, had already fallen apart under the increasing CCF pressure. Others, particularly the Capitol Division to the east, were holding well.

The withdrawal of some our units to the designated defensive line near Wonju proved to be surprisingly difficult because the Chinese were now threatening to encircle them as they attacked the south-bound convoys that were slowed by driving snow. On a smaller scale, they were facing the some of the same problems that we did during our disastrous retreat from Kunu-ri in North Korea a little over two months previously.

A battalion surgeon was said to have shot down, with his carbine, a Chinese soldier, only about twenty yards away from the road, who was trying to remove a gold wedding ring from the finger of a fallen GI. The Dutch battalion headquarters that had been trying to hold Hoensong sustained heavy casualties, including losing their commander, when they mistakenly identified a group of advancing Chinese as friendly ROKs.

The next day the perimeter defense around Wonju was completed. By now, many of the units involved were again significantly under-strength, but again a massive number of artillery outfits had been brought up to support our efforts to hold the lines. The enemy still seemed to not have much artillery. The sun was shining on that day, February the 11th, and it was clearly warmer. The chirping of rather mangy little sparrows in the barren trees seemed to be undeterred by the distant booming of guns.

A signal corps photographer came by to take pictures of our layout. He seemed most amused by our water purifier, a large canvas tank inside a tent, where we chlorinated water for use by the regiment. He was also interested in the fact that so many of us had shoulder holsters, me included, for our .45 automatic pistols. We had them made up in civilian shops when we were still down south while the regiment was being reorganized. He was even impressed by the Russian-made PPSh 7.62 mm "burp" gun that one of the infantry officers had given me. It was one of several that his company had captured from the North Koreans a few weeks earlier. The rapid-fire pieces were widely used by the NKPA infantry.

The North Koreans were said to be completely outfitted and supplied by the Russians. The Chinese Communist Forces, who only recently were said to have gotten any real support from the Russians, had a mixed bag of armaments. A lot were of American origin that had been captured when Chiang Kai-shek's Nationalist army had capitulated to the Chinese Communist army under Mao Tse-tung in 1949. They also had Japanese armament captured at the end of World War II. Instead of the Russian PPSh "burp" guns that the North Koreans were given, the Chinese infantry often had to make do with captured American Thompson sub-machine guns using box-type ammo clips rather than the more familiar, at least to us, drum type. This variety of weapons must have been something of a nightmare for Chinese supply officers.

We didn't know much about it at the time, but the Chinese and North Korean soldiers we were facing were not just hordes of simple peasants, but rather were hardened soldiers. Many had fought with the Russians and the Chinese during World War II, not to mention that those who fought with, as well as against, the Japanese. Indeed, we heard it said that some of the best of the South Korean generals were actually North Koreans with much the same backgrounds who had migrated to South Korea during the late 1940's, the gap between the end of World War II and the attack of the North Koreans in 1950.

I began seeing many of our older sergeants on sick call, each complaining of no longer being able to "do their jobs right," and seemed to imply that accordingly they should be reassigned to "more rearward" units. I didn't really know what to tell them. Bob Howard had little sympathy for them.

CHAPTER 18

When fighting erupted again to the north and west of Wonju, our division's sector continued to be relatively quiet. Eighth Army had issued orders that there would be no further withdrawals. Everyone had to stand and fight. We had no doubt that our regiment would soon be in the thick of it.

Indeed, on the 14th, we moved the collecting station up to Nodo-ri, closer to and south-southwest of Wonju. Our regiments had become deeply embroiled in the continuing battles for Wonju and were taking casualties. One of our regiments had become surrounded and cut off by a vastly superior force of CCF in a valley about 30 kilometers or so northwest of us.

Another regiment had a battalion that became literally chewed up, company by company. Of the 15 litter bearers out with that battalion, there was only one left. Despite heavy casualties again being incurred by the massed artillery in position near Wonju, the communist armies continued to press their attack, much aided by the return of a persistent cloud cover. This prevented not only aerial observation but also fighter plane support. It looked like the United Nations forces were becoming literally overwhelmed by what seemed like vastly superior numbers of enemy. In the often scatologically-shaded lingo of the GIs, the shit had really hit the fan. Denied our air support, it almost seemed as if we didn't have the manpower on the ground to carry the day against such a swarming and determined enemy.

However, in a couple of days near midnight, the clouds finally lifted, and the air force was able to go to work, even using flares to illuminate potential targets while it was still dark just before dawn. As soon as it was daylight many more planes were sent to bomb the Chinese and North Korean positions. Aerial re-supply was now possible for the beleaguered regiment northwest of us. Our new defensive positions also made it possible for helicopters, previously restricted by heavy enemy small arms fire, to again come in to help evacuate casualties.

Most of the division's combat outfits were continuing to take casualties as they tried to pull back and close in on their assigned defensive positions. Communications were frequently interrupted. While the intentions of the enemy were pretty well understood, what continued to surprise us was the sheer numbers of Chinese and North Koreans and how aggressive they were.

Despite having the technological advantages of airplanes, artillery, and tanks, as we did, it became very clear that there was still no substitute for foot soldiers on the ground. Perhaps our soldiers should be more like those of our enemies, stolid, well-trained, and obedient. We came to understand, if we hadn't already, why the Infantry was known as the "Queen of Battles."

With the break in the weather, our air support at last with us again, and our vast superiority in artillery, our under-strength outfits were finally again able to turn the tide a bit and make progress. Why the Chinese and the North Koreans still did not seem to have much artillery was undoubtedly the result of unopposed American aerial surveillance and effective air strikes along their long supply lines from their bases in the distant north.

While Operation Roundup had not turned out to be as successful as hoped, it was now thought that at least it seemed to have forced the enemy to go on the offensive before they were quite ready. As one of our officers put it, if that theory was correct, it could have been heaven help us if the "gooks" had had the time to get fully prepared.

Attempts to get through to the encircled regiment that had been holding out so valiantly were finally successful on the 16th. Our patrols were now reporting no contact with the enemy. Even so, the losses our division had sustained were awesome. One battalion was down to the effective strength of just one company. The situation, from the GIs' rather skeptical standpoint, was becoming the worst we had seen since the disastrous battles near Kunu-ri in North Korea.

Morale in our outfit was notably boosted when one of our sergeants, out with a battalion patrol west of Wonju, found the lid, rotor, and rollers of a Montgomery Ward washing machine on a rubbish pile. A search and rescue operation soon found the tub in our engineer battalion's area. A bottle of Canadian Club made the tub ours. The machine was soon reassembled, and working well, thanks to our newly acquired portable electric generator. The South Korean houseboys quickly learned how to use it.

CHAPTER 19

Regimental Headquarters was to move north the next day, the 17th of February, to a position closer to Wonju. The roads were still so bad, hopefully temporarily, that it was decided that the collecting station should stay where it was for the time being. We could easily hear the booming of artillery to the north, and we learned that there were reports of four new Chinese field armies heading down our way. Despite pessimistic predictions about how the war was going, it became apparent that the CCF we had been facing were now sliding off to the northwest. Things had quieted down considerably in the collecting station, and the weather turned a bit warmer again.

The rations continued to be notably improved. Our washing machine and the clean clothes it provided was much appreciated. We even had occasional surprisingly pleasant and a bit warmer sunny days, even if the temperatures still got down to well below freezing at night. While we knew that operational plans for further attacks against the enemy were in the works, everything remained reasonably quiet.

We amused ourselves by setting up empty fuel drums in draws in the nearby hills for target practice with our .45 automatics and carbines. We got to know the three regimental chaplains better when they enthusiastically joined us. While they did occasionally come around the Collecting Station, they seemed to spend most of their time out with the battalions, particularly when they were in combat. They also worked out of Regimental Headquarters, and our Collecting Station was often bivouacked at some distance from it. We all became friendly enough to even, from time to time, have a few of drinks together on the uncommon occasions when there was anything available to drink.

By the 20th, we were quite busy with processing many men now returning to duty from being hospitalized earlier in Japan. When we saw Marine truck convoys moving up the road that ran by our area, we realized that things would soon be getting active again. We also marveled at all the equipment the Marine outfits were hauling with them.

The next day was cooler and cloudy. Having at last received orders to displace, we got up early to pack up, strike camp, and move out. Being bivouacked so close to the road, we had been kept awake the previous night by the passing convoys of noisy Marine vehicles, particularly their tanks. Those convoys were long, and from the bumper markings on some of the trucks, it was apparent that a lot of Army vehicles were helping them move their gear. When Collecting's many loaded vehicles were finally lined up ready to go, we had to wait until MPs from Division showed up to enforce a break in traffic between the Marine convoy serials so that we could get our own rather long column of trucks and jeeps out on the rutted dirt road.

We headed north to Wonju, now blown even flatter and pockmarked with infinitely more shell craters. There were Marines and Marine vehicles all over the place. We then turned southeast to now-familiar Sillim-ni, a distance of about 18 kilometers, or 12 miles. Progress was slow over the poor roads.

As soon as we found our bivouac area and had set up our tents, a drenching and frigid downpour began. The adjacent untended rice paddies sopped it up and quickly became oleaginous. It took two truckloads of straw, gathered up from nearby abandoned haystacks, to put down on the earthen floors of our tents to make them habitable. We heard that a radio message from the Chinese in front of us had been intercepted, saying that they were running critically short of ammunition and were planning to withdraw even further.

While the rain still poured down, the Marines jumped off from their new positions ten miles northwest of us towards Hoensong to begin "Operation Killer." The next day an Army division jumped off to the east of Wonju and north of Chechon to pinch off an enemy salient into our lines that was left over from the recent communist offensive, and soon managed to surround an estimated 2000 to 10,000 Chinese and North Korean troops. Another American division was advancing further to the east of us, and beyond it the very effective ROK Capital Division was advancing. To the immediate west of us was another of our division's regiments and then another and less-effective ROK division, although it was partially screened by the Marines. It seemed like just about everyone was heading north again.

That night the wind came up and brought more heavy, freezing rain and winds while we were watching a rather forgettable motion picture starring Betty Grable in one of Regimental Headquarters' tents. We scrambled back to our area through the wind-driven downpour to arrive just in time to grab the squad tent that we used for receiving patients as it started to become air borne. After struggling with the tent for nearly an hour, we finally parked a 2 1/2 ton truck and tied the tent to it.

One of the problems was that we were short of tent pegs. However, the soft muddy ground provided only poor purchase for the ones we did have. In the morning we were literally surrounded by a sea of mud, but it did not prove to be a deterrent to a large sick call.

We soon moved again as our troops advanced, now up into a rather wild and desolate area in a valley crossed by several streams that were swollen by the recent rains. We became concerned that if said rains continued, those streams might soon swell even further and coalesce into large rivers or even lakes. The name of the place remained a mystery, and there were no villages of any size to be seen nearby. We decided to just call it "the boondocks." On a north-south line we were about level with Wonju and eleven miles, or 17 kilometers, northeast of Sillim-ni. Our battalions were soon dug in on the steep hills surrounding the valley.

Such as it was, the continuation of our main supply road, because of the overflowing streams, was frequently under water all the way to a "gang," or river, that was about two miles, or three kilometers, to the north. In the absence of a bridge, the swollen river was difficult to cross by any vehicles other than tanks. Nonetheless, our troops were probing to the north.

The line outfits had to contend with the fact that, beyond that point, there were almost no other roads at all, just more steep hills and valleys. The rain pretty much prevented using helicopters, since they didn't seem to be equipped for operation in bad weather. When it wasn't raining there was ice everywhere.

The only vehicles that could operate at all well in such circumstances were ones that had tracks, like tanks, so we used them for evacuating casualties. After tanks went over the muddy ground a few times, their weight could often compact the mud to the point of forming impromptu road surfaces that trucks could navigate, but only very slowly and carefully. A battalion was detached to bring up supplies to a place where a horde of native bearers supplied by Regiment could load them on A-frames and carry them on their backs up narrow winding trails through the hills to where the line outfits were dug in.

The major went back to Regimental Forward on the 26th while I stayed behind in Collecting to hold the fort. When the casualties from the forward units started flooding in at about 1600, we found that they had been evacuated from battalion aid stations as early as 1100 that day, which was how long it took the litter jeeps to reach us over the poor roads. It was fortunate that most of the casualties we were seeing were relatively lightly wounded. We realized that taking so long for the casualties to reach definitive care could undoubtedly result in many of the more seriously wounded dying along the way.

While the enemy seemed to have an abundant supply of small arms, machine guns, and mortars, they still didn't seem to have much artillery. Nonetheless, they were numerous, usually well dug in, and continued to put up a stubborn resistance. We had to wonder if that radio intercept about them being short of ammunition was little more than a devious plant.

CHAPTER 20

We didn't get through seeing wounded until 0300 the next morning, the 27th of February. Despite the delays due to the terrain and the miserable state of the roads, once casualties reached our collecting station they were treated and transferred to a Division clearing station fairly quickly. This had not always been the case, particularly during that ill-fated recent campaign into North Korea. The ambulance runs from our collecting station to a division medical clearing station had become much shorter than they so often were earlier in the war.

The day was relatively warm, and there were far fewer battle casualties, but this was more than made up for by our increasingly active sick call. There also was a continuous parade of wounded and captured North Koreans and Chinese soldiers being brought in. We continued to spray them all with DDT and inoculate them against typhus as soon as they darkened the tent entrance.

Sick call was becoming even more bizarre. GIs sent in from the battalion aid stations had some of the weirdest complaints I could ever imagine. While some of them, of course, were valid, it was all too clear that many other GIs were just hoping that the more outlandish their complaints were, the better chance they would have of being evacuated. Separating the two groups was wearying.

That night, after the last patient had been evacuated, someone suggested that we try making eggnog with medical alcohol. The result, to say the least, proved to be quite gratifying. We invited the chaplains, who soon confirmed our impression that they indeed were rather delightful guys.

The next day, Bill Sloan was still back with Regiment Forward, and all the other Collecting officers had been ordered down to Division Rear in Hamchang for Lieutenant Jones' preliminary hearing preparatory to being court-martialed. My memory of how Jones had tried to shoot Howard earlier in the month was still quite vivid. For a moment, I wondered why I hadn't been called to testify, but then realized that someone back in Division Rear must have understood that at least one medical officer had to stay with Collecting.

When taking care of evening sick call was finally completed, Capt. George MacDonald, the leader of the ambulance platoon supporting us, Lt. Archie Moreno, and I attacked a Gouda cheese that friends at home had sent me. Archie had been the sole survivor of his infantry company twice, so the higher-ups had finally concluded that he shouldn't push his luck any further. He was staying with us while awaiting reassignment to a rear area.

The next day, the last in February, was overcast. Sick call was again something akin to a theatre of the absurd. The complaints continued to be mostly reiterative, almost as if the GIs presenting them had discussed them amongst themselves beforehand. Our collecting station medics who would first screen, or triage, the walk-in sick call tended to get rather hard-nosed about dealing with them. I had to keep an eye on them to make sure they wouldn't be turning away men who really had valid complaints. Of course, we had no choice but to ultimately send the malingerers back to duty.

When sick call was finally dealt with, I managed to take a shower at a nearby Corps shower unit that had just set up near us. As I stood under the spray, I began to remember what it had been like to take a shower with my young wife. This led me to wondering again about where in the hell was that replacement that I was so eager to welcome. Since

John Benton

the weather continued to be warmer, I decided to dispense with the long john underwear bottoms when I got dressed, hoping that I was not being overly optimistic about the Korean weather.

On the clear and windy first day of March, the regiment received almost 200 replacements, all enlisted men. They were quite remarkable in that so few of them made sick call their first stop. We were now getting called–up reservists and men who had been drafted. They seemed to have been much better trained before being sent to South Korea.

I was still the only officer in the collecting station. It was fortunate that we were not receiving many casualties, and as had become usual, most of the ones we did see didn't get to us until relatively late in the day.

Since it was also payday time, I was asked to be the pay officer for the Medical Company, involving dispensing about $14,000. It would have meant not only paying the men in the collecting station, but also going out to the three battalion aid stations to oversee the paying of their personnel. Still the only medical officer in Collecting, I was able to beg off. The rest of our officers would be back from Ed Jones' court hearing at Division Rear the next day.

Actually, no real money was involved, since we were paid by military script in dollar denominations. When the troops were not in actual combat and in reserve status, they might spend it for local goods and services, the latter quite often being temporary female companionship whenever they could find it. Every once in a while the military script would be changed quite suddenly and without any prior warning. This would render previous script versions instantly worthless and diminish the threat of counterfeiting.

Only two casualties came in that evening. One GI had somehow managed to drive his jeep into a tree, although with little damage to its occupants. As a result, I had more of a chance to sit and chat with some of our collecting station personnel, all regular Army, and get to know them better.

What I had long suspected turned out to be true. Just about all of them at one time or another had had run-ins with the law in civilian life, although with little prison time. It was mostly things like drunken driving and statutory rape. Nonetheless, almost all of them were very competent medics. Perhaps enlisting in the Army had been good for them.

It was even colder the next day thanks to a snow flurry. There was an unusually large number of GIs on sick call. As usual, there were more than a few that we suspected of malingering. The line battalions were still plowing their way north through rough country, to the extent that we often still had to rely on tracked vehicles to bring out the wounded. That night it was clear, cold, again with gusting winds that played hell with our tents. I decided that I'd better put my long john bottoms back on.

The first of our MSC officers to return from the court martial instantly got the job of paymaster. I received my usual monthly stipend in military script, that is, what was left over after the deduction of what was automatically sent home.

CHAPTER 21

We packed up and moved out to the east the next day to keep up with our battalions. They were now swinging over that way to help pinch off what remained of the enemy salient. This was to be the first of several campaigns to methodically knock out as many of the enemy as possible, and was called "Operation Ripper." We were still in rough country with very poor roads.

There was a tragic incident in another regiment when five rounds from a battery of 155 mm howitzers fell several hundred yards short of their intended target. Two company commanders and sixty or seventy men were taken out.

We finally bivouacked near a town that we thought was called Sangju-ri, near a river about 25 miles east of Wonju, but we weren't really certain. Our maps, mostly based on ones made by the Japanese when they occupied Korea, were reasonably accurate about the locations of little towns, but they often didn't have the names quite right. We were not far from yet another river.

Fires caused by the day's air strikes and artillery barrages still burned on distant hillsides. As it got darker, a sergeant from one of our regimental tanks brought us a message they had received on their radio about a 3/4 ton Heavy Weapons truck that had hit a land mine down near the river and that there were casualties. One of our medics promptly notified the nearest battalion aid station to send out a couple of litter jeeps.

Two hours later, one of the men that had been riding in the truck but was not injured walked in, apparently having hitched a ride, and reported that there was one man who couldn't walk. He said that the rest were holed up in a native hut near the river with three other GIs. He hadn't seen any sign of a litter jeep, and as far as he knew the road was still clear. When we tried again to get in touch by field telephone with that nearest battalion aid station, we still couldn't raise them, I sent now-Sergeant Gonzales out with one of our litter jeeps. He soon returned, reporting that he couldn't get through on the road because the Chinese had put in a roadblock. Since he was one of our old-timers, I couldn't really blame him for becoming a bit cautious.

Bob Howard called Regiment to find out about the roadblock, and was told that a platoon had already been dispatched to eliminate it. I related this to Gonzales and told him to go back, and as soon as the road was clear, go on and see if he could find the hut near the river before it got too dark. He could always ask for directions.

About this time two enlisted men leading two dozen new replacements came by, wanting to find out what we knew about the roads out to one of the battalions. When I told them that we didn't know much except that there might still be a gook roadblock, one of the leaders wanted to know if they could get a tank to accompany them. I had to point out that all of our tanks were already very busy backing up our troops on the line.

Then, another GI, almost out of breath, came in to report that the native hut where the casualties from the damaged 3/4 ton truck were holed up had been sprayed with fire from some of the enemy that had established the roadblock. The occupants of the hut had all bailed out the door and taken cover in the nearby shrubbery. He said that there were actually nine casualties in all, only one non-ambulatory, and that the roadblock had finally been eliminated. The disparate reports of how many wounded there were was not unusual.

Then, three more of them, not severely wounded, walked in. Gonzalez soon returned with a wounded young lieutenant on his litter jeep who had been leading the group and was the non-ambulatory casualty. We soon had them all patched up and sent on their way to Clearing. I don't think we ever did get the details sorted out about exactly what had happened.

The next day, March 4th, was warmer again with lots of sunshine, and the frozen ground around us again soon became a vast sea of mud. We received a badly wounded man, with almost countless bullet holes and only barely alive. While we worked almost frantically controlled the bleeding, we had to make an incision in his arm to find a vein so we could start some plasma on him, the peripheral ones having all collapsed because his blood volume was so depleted. At first he looked better. However, as we were loading him into an ambulance, he took a turn for the worse. Plasma could temporarily replace fluid volume, but it was only a temporary substitute for whole blood, which then was available only as far forward as the division clearing stations. We tried artificial respiration, but it was to no avail, so we had to pronounce him dead.

Then, we heard the distinctive sound of a "chopper," an evacuation helicopter, landing on the flat ground to the west of our area. This was something we hadn't seen very often, since the choppers seemed to work mostly between the clearing stations and the MASH outfits. In those days, they came out to the battalion or regimental areas only after a specific request had been made for one, and sometimes only after said request was processed through several ascending levels of Army bureaucracy before being granted. This way of doing things was, of course, soon to be simplified.

It turned out that a battalion of a nearby infantry division had gotten into a severe firefight and had taken a lot of casualties. Because they couldn't use the road back to their collecting station because of the mud in their area, they were bringing their patients to our area in their litter jeeps. We would process them in our collecting station and then evacuate them to our clearing station since we could use the roads in our area. The helicopter had come in to help evacuate the more serious cases.

Almost all of the casualties we received, including two KATUSAs, were severely injured, and one of them was pronounced dead soon after being placed in a chopper's evacuation pod. Because of all the other wounded to be evacuated, we picked up the covered body from pod and carried it to one side of a tent. After doing several emergency chest wound closures, we evacuated the two most severely injured men by the chopper, and sent the others on back to our clearing station by our ambulances, our road to the rear still being reasonably passable.

Later, while we were still busy, one of the sergeant technicians came up to tell me that the man we had earlier pronounced dead and had set off to one side on a litter under a blanket was breathing. The medics had carried him back inside our receiving tent. I ran over to see for myself. The body was cold, the pupils were dilated, there was no pulse and no audible heart beat. It was apparent that he was just having agonal chest spasms that can mimic breathing as rigor mortis sets in. He had suffered a massive abdominal wound with massive blood loss that was certain to be fatal in those days.

After the body was again carried back outside, we finally had a chance to sit down for a moment. One of the regimental chaplains, Captain Bob Riley, who now often worked with us when we were getting in casualties, checked the man's dog tags, found them engraved with a "C" for Roman Catholic, and pronounced the church's Last Rites. We then took out our pipes. After lighting them, we began chatting about the vagaries of fate.

It hadn't been many minutes before Sgt. Henderson breathlessly came into the tent to announce that the "body" was breathing again. I responded that what they were seeing was undoubtedly only agonal spasms. Nonetheless, I followed the sergeant back to the tent. It was the damnedest thing, in that it really did look like the corpse was breathing, although everything else pointed to death. To give the poor guy the benefit of the doubt, we quickly put him in an ambulance that was just leaving. Since Graves Registration didn't seem to operating at the moment in our area, we also loaded the other body into the ambulance. I wasn't at all surprised to hear that when it arrived at the Clearing Station, both bodies were promptly pronounced as dead.

The mud soon froze, making ordinary vehicular transport easier. Then, we were ordered to douse some of our lights. It was thought that the inevitable light leaks from our tent entrances as we moved litters in and out were too likely to draw enemy sniper fire. We had been too busy to be aware of it.

CHAPTER 22

March 6th was initially a relatively quiet day for us, although later there was a very sad aspect. Charley Morse dropped by our tent in the afternoon to ask if we needed anything special from Regimental Supply since he was heading that way. I answered that, for the moment, we were okay.

Soon after Charley left, Bob Howard called the officers together away from the tents and the other personnel, and rather quietly told us that Division had just called to tell him that Charley, perhaps the hardest working of any of us, was being ordered back to Division Rear for a preliminary hearing that could lead to a court martial.

He had always been a rather reticent sort of a man who kept pretty much to himself, but was well liked by our enlisted men. In retrospect, I suppose he was a bit different from the other officers, but perhaps it was masked by the way he was always so very diligent in performing his duties.

We now learned that a young sergeant in one of the line companies had registered a complaint nearly a month previously with Division Rear accusing Charley of having sexually assaulted him, or as it was officially described, "made improper advances." Exactly what the sergeant's role had been in the matter was unclear. Also noted was that Charley was believed to have had what was then called "homosexual panic" as factor in the case, which none of us really understood. It all came as a surprise. We hadn't noticed anything really peculiar in his behavior. As a supply officer, he was, of course, often away from Collecting and in other areas.

After a rather quiet inquiry, Division had decided that the charges were worthy of investigation. The preliminary hearing that he was facing could lead to a court-martial. In consideration of his otherwise excellent service record, the case might be dismissed, but it was more likely that the best outcome he could expect would be a quiet discharge from the Army.

There were, to be sure, occasional rumors going around about homosexual activity. It was considered to be no less than criminal behavior. Such activity may have been more widespread than we ever realized because most of those involved were probably very discreet. We decided that we would say nothing about the matter for the moment to the enlisted men, although the ever-present Army rumor mill would undoubtedly pick up on it soon enough.

We also recognized that we were losing a good soldier and officer. It somehow did not seem quite fair. But, regulations were regulations. The next day, Charley Morse managed to quietly slip away without saying goodby to any of us.

I realized that the calm would not last. Indeed, our still half-strength line outfits were ordered to jump off the next day. They initially met little resistance from the enemy, but we still worried about the ROK divisions on our flanks. While we were still receiving casualties, by the 9th our line companies had advanced to what seemed like the enemy's main line of resistance. While dealing with many casualties, we all were concerned about how soon the enemy might turn and counter-attack, and how massive that effort might be. Tanks still often had to be used for evacuating the wounded because of the persistent mud during the warmer days.

Most unexpectedly, we were sent four pints of whole blood, previously seldom, if ever, seen forward of a Division clearing station. I wished that we could have had it two days previously. The life of the severely wounded man brought in then might have been saved, or at least we could have gotten him down to Clearing with enough life left in him for more definitive care.

I was ordered to make a "house call" on the commanding general of one of the ROK divisions on our right flank. Eighth Army apparently had learned that said general was ill, and had notified Corps, who in turn called our division, and ultimately the job of doing something about it was handed down to me. I was driven in one of our litter jeeps some eight kilometers down a lateral road to the headquarters of the ROK division. It took us a while to find the general. When we finally did, he was standing by the side of the road surrounded by his headquarters staff and his American advisors from the Korean Military Advisory Group that were assigned to his division. He was quite polite, and said that, yes, yesterday he had felt sick, but today he felt fine.

Our too often more than a little reluctant GIs had thought up another rather ingenious way of getting off the front lines. It was to slip off at night with their pockets full of C-rations and hide in an abandoned native hut for at least three days, then come in claiming that they had escaped after being captured, or had been captured and turned loose. We would then have to evacuate them as escaped Prisoners of War.

However, one who tried it was caught with a letter from a buddy of his with specific instructions about how to go about doing it. The buddy had apparently gotten away with it himself a few weeks previously. It was becoming more and more difficult to stay ahead of the "gold bricks."

CHAPTER 23

By the 11th of March we had moved north to an area about 15 kilometers east of Hoensong, and about the same distance north of Wonju. Again, we weren't sure what the place was called; it was simply described by map coordinates. Our troops, still advancing, were at times taking rather heavy casualties when they encountered small but well-entrenched and stubborn groups of enemy. We were being kept busy most days until well after midnight.

A particularly serious case was that of a young GI from the Heavy Mortar section who accidentally set off a hand grenade. He sustained several severe wounds, any one of which could probably have been enough to kill him. He died before we could evacuate him.

We learned that rotation plans had been formally announced by both the Marines and their Navy medical support units. The only news of any such action by the Army still seemed to amount to little more than rumors that such a policy was being considered. However, despite our proximity to the front lines, we were still having a motion picture show when circumstances permitted, and of course enjoyed the convenience of having a Corps shower unit available to us every once in a while.

The next day, a Sunday, was rather nice. The fighting had slackened off. There wasn't much sick call. After a morning church service, in the afternoon I visited two of our battalion aid stations as well as the shower unit. We even had roast beef with Yorkshire pudding for dinner.

One of our regiments reached our next objective, the Albany Line above Yudong-ni, the following day. Mud was again complicating things as were the land mines now being left by the retreating CCF. When the ground was dry they were usually visible since they were mostly mortar shells that had been left semi-buried in the ground with their noses sticking up. Where the surface was muddy or covered with snow, their noses would often sink out of sight, but they were potentially just as lethal.

The other two regiments of our division were still doing most of our Division's fighting, and had already reached the Reno line. However, we knew that we would be again moving north soon enough. A tough fight was expected when the troops attempted to take over a mountain pass along the Yudong-ni-Pungam-ni road in order to reach the Idaho line, our next objective. At least for the moment the enemy seemed to have melted away from the sector directly in front of us.

On March 11th we moved the collecting station up to the vicinity of yet another clump of miserable and deserted little farmers' hovels that we thought constituted a village named Sokpokol, although again we weren't too sure. It was about midway between Hoensong and Hongchon. We shared a rather pretty little valley with five artillery batteries that seemed bent on keeping up the noise level. It was hilly country with only a few winding dirt roads that were barely passable for our motor vehicles even when dry. Bringing up supplies was a challenge.

As we were getting closer to the 38th parallel, the arbitrary line that had divided North and South Korea after the end of World War II, we kept wondering if we would be sent north of it again. We also wondered if the CCF and the NKPA were planning to make stands on that parallel. The weather continued to be fairly nice, and a bit warmer, which made the beer rations that we were beginning to get in more frequently all the more enjoyable.

We celebrated St. Patrick's Day by another tedious move through rather picturesque country up to the vicinity of Pungnam-ni. It appeared to have once been a fairly good-sized town, but like so many others, civilians had deserted it and it subsequently had been mostly leveled into piles of ruble. Our chosen bivouac site was in another pleasant valley about 1000 meters north of the town, behind a hill. Many of the adjacent hills had been intricately honeycombed with trenches and pillboxes by the enemy before they pulled back, but, for some reason, had apparently never been used for combat purposes. We were about 500 meters behind the positions being held by an ROK division.

We had creamed eggs on toast for breakfast the next morning, the 18th of March, and also Palm Sunday. The weather continued to be fine, if cool, now with little snow in sight except on the highest hills. Since our troops had not been hitting much, sick call was quickly done. We had roast turkey for lunch.

A GI came in that afternoon complaining of a cold, but upon listening to his chest, I discovered that he had a heart murmur. I thought it might not be of too much significance, but sent him back to Clearing for them to check him out. We had steak for dinner, reminding me that I was now eating a great deal better than I usually did at the university hospital where I had been an intern. We all continued to give General Ridgway the credit for the improvement in our rations, as well as a much improved command structure.

That night, it turned colder. We had a double feature of movies, "The Hit Parade of 1951," and "Buccaneer Girl," both pretty ho-hum. I had never before realized that Hollywood had been cranking out so many "B" movies for the "double features" at the movie theaters that were then so popular. Even if we seemed doomed to see just about all of them, we were grateful to have them.

When the little stove in our tent suddenly stopped functioning just after midnight, I was soon shivering even in my Arctic sleeping bag, and I could only wonder how

Success to Stalemate in South Korea

the GIs of the line companies out in their foxholes were doing.

In the morning, Sloan and I were the last to leave the mess tent after breakfast. It turned out to be a bright, clear day, although still quite chilly. The hills bordering the valley were starting to change from a uniform dull brown to having patches of green that heralded the rather slow arrival of spring, at least where they hadn't been blackened by napalm.

As we got up from the table I heard what sounded like a low-flying jet aircraft.

Sloan turned and said, "What the hell is that?"

"Sounds like one of our new fighter jets," I answered.

"Maybe it's a gook plane."

I shook my head. "Since we don't have any air bases this far north, it's more likely to be one of our guys in trouble."

Once outside the tent, we joined several of our medics who were looking intently to the west where a plane was circling at a low altitude.

"He could be looking for a place to make an emergency landing," I said.

"Or it could be a gook looking for something to shoot up," Sloan replied.

"No," I replied, "it looks more like one of those new Lockheed jet fighters."

"You're sure it's not one of those Russian MiGs the gooks fly?"

"Pretty sure. If he's looking for a place to make an emergency landing, I don't know where he could find one around here."

Sloan shaded his eyes with his hand. "It looks like he's coming down over that cross road south of us. I can see that the plane doesn't have a red star on it, so I guess you're right, he's probably one of ours. Could he land there?"

"If he can find a long enough piece of straight road, he might be able to stall it in and belly land with his landing gear up."

"Maybe we should grab a jeep and go see what's happening."

"Good idea," I said, as we simultaneously started to run towards a litter jeep parked near by. I jumped in the driver's seat, and as Sloan climbed into the passenger's seat, I started up the engine, checked the fuel gauge, and made a wide circle to get headed around towards the north-south road near us.

Sgt. Henderson came running out of the receiving tent and flagged us down, shouting that an artillery outfit about a mile behind us had called in, saying that a plane had just crashed near their positions and was on fire. I waved as we increased our speed and turned to head south towards the crossroad. It wasn't long after we turned onto it that we could see a column of smoke to the east, and soon came upon the burning wreckage of the plane off to the side of the road in a field.

Already a few men, probably from nearby units, were running towards the crashed plane. It was easy to see what had happened. The pilot had apparently tried to belly in on one of the few reasonably wide fields alongside the road.

"What a mess," Sloan said, as I parked the jeep by the side of the road. "He might have made it okay if it hadn't been for those two stone walls."

"He probably couldn't see them because of how high the weeds have grown," I replied, as we climbed out of the jeep. "There's also a lot of big rocks in that field that he probably couldn't see."

It looked like the pilot had attempted a gear up landing while still carrying a good turn of speed, and after touching down plowed a deep furrow in the uneven ground, crossed a stream, gone on through the two stone walls and shed parts for at least another 500 feet.

"Maybe he was low on of fuel," I said. "The fires are already almost out."

"I wonder what happened to him." Sloan he lit a cigarette.

"He could have been coming back from a mission up north, and if it wasn't that he was low on fuel, maybe he was badly wounded and died."

"How can an all-metal plane burn like that?"

"Probably because of magnesium alloys in it's structure," I answered. "If they get hot enough, they can catch fire. Jet fuel can burn pretty hot."

Sloan grunted, and said, "Maybe we better go see about the pilot."

"Or what's left of him," I replied.

We had to push our way through those arriving spectators to get to the plane. For once I was glad that we were again wearing our insignia of rank and branch of service so that we were readily identifiable as medical officers.

The canopy over the cockpit had been torn away. It didn't take us long to find the remains of the pilot in the cockpit. However, all that was recognizable was a blackened torso and head that were only vaguely human, with only stumps remaining of what had been arms and legs. The impact might have killed him if he wasn't already dead, or maybe he had been wounded and died in the very hot fuel-driven fire. His restraint harness hadn't been unfastened. His dogtags were intact and hanging on their chain around his neck.

Sloan bent over, and as he straightened up, he said, "Couldn't he have ejected and come down by his parachute?"

"He was probably too low to do that," I replied, "maybe because he'd been wounded and couldn't really control the plane, or maybe he was already dead. Maybe that was why he was unable to realize when he got closer to the ground that he'd picked the wrong place for an emergency landing."

Sloan shook his head. "Maybe it isn't so bad to be in the infantry after all."

I almost wanted to laugh, as I said, "That's probably debatable."

CHAPTER 24

So many of our medics, just like so many other GIs, seemed to continue having problems, or at least what they perceived as being problems, with their wives and girlfriends back in the States. Many of them had probably grown tired of waiting and wanted to get on with their lives. Perhaps it had always been this way, when men were off fighting an unpopular war with little civilian support. It wasn't just the enlisted men and the non-coms, even some of our commissioned officers were also having their problems. I did the best I could when they sought my advice, but of course, I could really do little more than just commiserate with them. It was perhaps all too evident that absence does not necessarily make the heart grow fonder.

Division Forward was, for once, bivouacked quite close to us, really no more than a kilometer back down the road. That afternoon, while all was still quiet, I decided to take a walk to visit the aid station there. Our battalion aid stations hadn't been getting in any casualties, and we had finished sick call for the regimental-level outfits by noon.

The medical officer, an old friend, and two MSC officers were sitting around their otherwise empty aid station tent and having a few beers since their beer ration, this time supplied by the Pabst brewery, had just come in. I joined them, sat down on the end of a cot, loaded my pipe, and hefted a can offered me along with what we called a "church key" to open it. The topic of conversation quickly turned to the prospects for rotation.

George MacDonald was also there, since his ambulance company was based nearby. He reminded me and my medical officer friend that he owed me a bottle of Scotch, and as soon as we finished our beers, invited the two of us to come over to one of the ambulances parked nearby to pick it up.

When we got to the ambulance, he opened up the back doors and invited me in. Considering that the ambulance body that could hold four litters was on the same chassis as were the Dodge 3/4 ton "Heavy Weapons" trucks, it seemed surprisingly roomy. He fished out three cans of beer from an ammunition box under a litter and handed one to each of us.

We sat across from each other on the lower two litters and proceeded to kill our beers while he regaled us with stories about his hobby of restoring old cars. Perhaps my friend and I were the only people around who had the patience to sit still and listen to him, but after all, it was his beer we were drinking. Division Forward's whisky ration had also belatedly just come in, which was how he was able to repay me with a bottle of Scotch for one that I had previously loaned him. We didn't often have the occasion, much less the opportunity, to do much drinking.

Then, an MSC major I knew from the Division Surgeon's office happened to walk by, and stopped when he saw us in the back of the ambulance. He quickly accepted George's invitation to join us, and proved to be quite willing to assist us in our efforts to deplete the local beer supply. He, too, was worrying about rotation, and also had heard nothing more about any Army plans for such a program for the MSC officers. All my friend and I could do was to commiserate with him.

That night, when the mail arrived, there was a package from my wife that also contained a new Kaywoodie pipe and a large tin of Doniford pipe tobacco. We also got in a generous supply of writing paper and envelopes from

Regiment, both almost always in short supply, this time courtesy of Budweiser.

On the next day, March 20th, a patrol from one of our battalions reached the Texas Line, another of the key objectives of "Operation Ripper," with little interference from the enemy. Things were still quiet, perhaps too much so.

An MSC captain from Eighth Army personnel dropped by, inquiring about the non-battle casualties we'd had, and whether we thought that any of them were due to defects in their training. He was also concerned about all the frostbite cases during the colder winter months that had ultimately led to a lot of amputations of toes.

Many of those cases, I explained, were the result of GIs out in the line companies wearing the troublesome Shoe-pacs that were actually designed for even colder weather than we had been having up in North Korea. With warmer weather, the troops had gone back to wearing the regular issue boots, which, of course, pretty much resolved the problem. I was all too well aware of the problems with those Shoepacs, because I, too, had been wearing them.

I also had to tell him about the gunshot wounds in the lower extremities we had been seeing, particularly earlier in the war, that we suspected were probably self-inflicted. He nodded, and said that other outfits had been having exactly the same problems, and that GIs who might have witnessed such actions were entirely unlikely to ever squeal on their buddies. And, of course, a lot of the accidents involving motor vehicles that caused so many of the non-battle casualties, were often the result of carelessness, stupidity, or both.

The next couple of days were uneventful. Some of us had time to hike over some hills to a nearby miserable little village where some refugees and their families were near starving. We carried a pile of C-rations with us. One of our Korean house boys came along to translate.

The refugees were a pitiful lot, all bundled up in clothing that looked like it was fast turning into rags. They told us, through our translator, that they had nearly run out of food, and were very appreciative of the rations we had brought them. They also told us that they were fearful of GIs, since they knew of at least three young girls within their own group who, in recent weeks, had been forcibly raped by them. We tried to apologize as best we could. As for trying to identify the miscreants, perhaps predictably, they couldn't even tell us what outfits the GIs were from.

I had to wonder if it the current rather quiet period was in fact the calm before the storm. I had decided to write up two papers to send to the medical training outfit at Fort Sam Houston in Texas. My efforts were hindered by the fact that our little typewriter had again become non-functional. Dumping it in a bucket of gasoline had helped a little, particularly after we then soaked it in gun oil, although it soon stiffened up again.

Later that afternoon, we had our medics assemble in the main tent so Bob Howard could explain to them the tactical military situation we were facing with "Operation Ripper." Keeping the troops aware and up to date of the "big picture" of what was going on in the war was a new idea and now considered to be very important for bolstering and maintaining their morale. Everything had been going rather well so far and assigned objectives were being reached. Bob then led an open discussion about the operation's significance, even if our regiment hadn't been nearly as active in it as were the other two in the division. Anyhow, for the moment, everything seemed to be proceeding reasonably well.

We were again experiencing monumental problems with mud everywhere, thanks to the recurrent and persistent spring rains. Bringing up supplies in wheeled vehicles as well as even moving around on foot had again often become difficult. A couple of M39s with their twin 40mm Bofors guns and tank-like tracks were temporarily assigned to our collecting station. Originally used for anti-aircraft duty, the arrival of jet military aircraft after WW II had rendered them obsolete, along with the half-tracked M16s with their quad .50 caliber machine gun turrets. Both vehicles had found new lives in being used mainly as mobile light artillery in support of infantry actions. The M39s were also often used for carrying ammunition and troops. Just about the smoothest riding vehicles we had, they worked well for evacuating casualties through the mud.

That night, I was invited to join a rather impromptu group in a battalion aid station's tent. Also included were the battalion surgeon, his MSC officer, Sloan and a couple of the line company commanders. Off the line in regimental reserve and bivouacked near their regimental headquarters area, the aid station people had somehow managed to acquire a few bottles of whisky. Soon fancying ourselves as a singing ensemble, we were reported to have kept people awake at a range of 300 meters and scared the hell out of the South Koreans in the vicinity, who thought they were hearing Chinese warming up for a Banzai attack. The occasion was my birthday, on the second day of spring.

The next day, a new rumor spread rapidly throughout the division. It was to the effect that our division would soon be stripped of all personnel with less than six months service time in Korea. They would then be transferred to other outfits. GIs from other infantry divisions that had been in Korea for more than six months would then be transferred to our division. It would then be replaced by another infantry division just coming into South Korea. Our reconstituted division would then be returned to the States. All of this was supposed to take place around the 15th of April. The rumor seemed much too good to be true, which, alas, proved to be correct.

We also learned that the airborne division had made a combat jump just north of Seoul. Line outfits were reported to have advanced up to a point only about 15 kilometers south of the 38th Parallel. We were also to move north the next day. That night, our movie was "All the King's Men." I thought it was one of the best I'd seen in Korea.

CHAPTER 25

Our move the next morning was up to the vicinity of Nabonni, a distance of only five or six kilometers. It was slowed by the need to ford a river, always a slow process for a convoy of vehicles like ours. The hills that surrounded it were very steep. Many of them still had parched and blackened areas from napalm air drops, although others were already showing touches of exuberant greenery. The rather pretty little valley, in many ways, reminded me of the Big Tujunga Canyon area in the foothills north of Los Angeles. A Corps shower unit chose to set up near our bivouac area.

As the day wore on, it became warm enough to roll up the sides of our tents. After we got things organized, I commandeered a jeep, refused the offer of a driver for it, and drove out to briefly visit our two battalion aid stations that were on the line. As I drove along, it was clear that things were turning green everywhere. Spring was definitely on the way. Our line companies, now dug in close to the 38th Parallel, were taking only occasional casualties, mostly on their patrols.

After dinner, several of us climbed an adjacent hill. From the top, we could see that the terrain for miles in front of us was mountainous. Back in our tent after dark, we wondered if we could dye up some hand grenades to mimic Easter eggs, since the next day would be Easter Sunday. That night we had a very good picture to watch called "State Secret," a British import.

It drizzled pretty much all of the next day. Since we were still seeing only a few casualties, some of us thought we might take a more extensive tour of the adjacent hills, a plan that was later cancelled. Most of us wound up attending an Easter church service conducted by the regimental chaplains.

A small Special Services entertainment group stopped by in the early afternoon. They were composed of a country singer called "Grandpappy Jones," with two female singers, all three playing electric guitars. It was said that they had achieved some degree of fame in the States on the radio. At the time, we considered them to be "hillbilly" singers. I wasn't much into that sort of music, and seriously even doubted that the word music was appropriate to describe the cacophony of sounds that they produced. Nonetheless, they had to be admired for making the trip all the way into the god-forsaken boondocks of South Korea to entertain us. They also went out to one of our battalions to do a show.

The major and I had found it increasingly necessary to adopt what we considered to be a hard-nosed attitude that gave short shrift to GIs, officers as well as enlisted men, who would repeatedly show up on sick call with nebulous complaints. We both realized that one could not be a very successful doctor at any level in civilian life with such an attitude. But, then again, this was the Army. Even so, I found myself wondering whether it was really such a smart idea for us to continue to implicitly assume that if we couldn't readily identify reasons for a GI's complaints, then they must be all in his head.

On March 27th, it took the Collecting Station convoy nearly 12 hours of stop and go driving to move 20 kilometers, or about 13 miles, up to the vicinity of Hangyi. The roads, not unexpectedly, were awful. By the time we were finally all set up in our assigned bivouac area and could hit the sack, as we referred to our sleeping bags, it was 0100 the next day. The heavily-damaged little town nearby was only about 19 kilometers south of the 38th Parallel. Many other army units were located near us.

I was able to visit a Marines' regimental medical unit that was on our regiment's left flank. The trip wasn't too easy because of the condition of the roads and frequent need to ford streams. However, I was able to spend some time talking to the regimental surgeon in charge of the unit.

It was immediately apparent that their set up was notably less luxurious, if such a word was at all appropriate, than was our collecting station, although they were as well equipped medically. They had the usual seven helicopters available that the Marines assigned to each of their regiments when on the line. We, in the Army, still thought we were doing well when we had two or three helicopters available to a regiment.

All of the personnel in the medical units supporting the Marines, the medical officers and the medical technicians, often called "corpsmen," were from the US Navy. The regimental surgeon, in the regular Navy, told me that he had been assigned to the Fleet Marines for seven years beginning in World War II. He had yet to see any duty in a military hospital. We got to talking about the differences between how the Marines and the Army fed their troops.

Our infantry line companies and other attached units such as the artillery battalion and the tank company each had their own mess kitchens, as did battalion and regimental headquarters units. They could often feed their men hot meals even when they were on the line and in combat. Otherwise, we ate C-rations.

Introduced during WW II, they came in a cardboard package a little bigger than a cigar box, and were supposed to supply enough nutrition for one man for one day in combat. Their contents, in little dark green cans, included one of a choice of several meat dishes and vegetable dishes. There were also little packets of water purification tablets, cookies, powdered instant coffee, creamer, cigarettes, moisture-resistant matches, jam, cocoa, beverage powder, a can opener, sugar, salt, pepper, toilet paper, and even chewing gum. It was said that if all the food in a box was consumed, it would amount to about 2500 calories.

C-rations were very useful for feeding troops in the field away from mess facilities. However, they were undeniably monotonous.

In Korea, the Marines were utilized more like regular infantry, except, of course, for their famous assault landing at Inchon in September, 1950. Their role in World War II, notably in the Pacific Theater, was as assault troops to take over Japanese-controlled islands. When the Marines were in action, the officers from the generals on down would often also go on C-rations. They didn't think they had any right to live better than their troops did, which certainly helped morale. Such an idea never seemed to gain much popularity with their opposite numbers in the Army. It was only when they were in reserve that the Marines could finally set up their battalion-sized messes and eat regular meals.

The rotation program that the Marines and Navy had set up for their men was already in operation. We were inclined to think that the Army's efforts so far to establish such a program amounted to little more than dithering. However, we also recognized that the Army had to deal with a far more complicated situation.

Treating sore feet

Sometimes we had to walk

Military haircut

Moving Up

**The Main Suplly Route for two
U.S. Army Divisions**

Helicopter evacuation of wounded

Tanks as ambulances during winter

Chow line

CHAPTER 26

By March 28th, our collecting station still hadn't been ordered to move further forward, perhaps because we were soon scheduled to go into Army reserve. This, of course, caused our litter jeep runs from the battalion aid stations to become longer, although, for the moment, we weren't receiving many casualties. Other than the patients sent back to us from the aid stations, the GIs that we were seeing on sick call were mostly from regiment-level and attached units. There were no longer many KATUSAs in our ranks.

It was anticipated that, once in reserve, we would have a good deal of hard work ahead of us in order to complete the indoctrination and integration of the many replacements we were told we would soon be receiving. We wondered, rather hopefully, if we medical officers might soon be offered rotation temporarily to military hospitals in Japan as we waited for rotation to the States.

At least, the weather was warmer, even if the pesky rains were constantly recurring. The next day, instead of moving back to go into reserve, our line companies were assigned to working on the nearby roads to help the combat engineers. Sick call was light.

The medical officer with an artillery battalion dropped by that afternoon. Things also quiet out his way. His purpose was to get some vitamin tablets, which we duly provided him. He was an interesting person. A German

Success to Stalemate in South Korea

doctor who had survived three years in Nazi concentration camps during WW II, he had later immigrated to the States and soon became an American citizen.

While we were chatting, a young man dressed in the uniform of the French battalion dropped in. He had been passing by, and came in to see our set-up. We soon found out that he was a Nigerian, and in addition to his native tongue, spoke a weird combination of French, German, and some English, with a scattering of Korean words.

Of course, the GIs, particularly when in the presence of Koreans, had their own curious patois of English, Japanese, and Korean. All Koreans had been forced to learn Japanese during the four decades of the Japanese occupation that ceased with the end of World War II. The GIs serving in the outfits that had been stationed in Japan during the subsequent peace-time years before the Korean War often had learned a lot of Japanese, particularly from their Japanese girlfriends. It was surprising how fast the rest of us picked up on the lingo even if we didn't have any compliant musames to help us.

We were soon communicating reasonably successfully with the Nigerian. His comments, perhaps best described as bitching, were virtually indistinguishable from those of the average American GI. He assured us that in all of Africa, as far as he knew, there was no place less desirable to be than anywhere in Korea. He also noted that the men of the French battalion were all convinced that as soon as our forces reached the 38th Parallel all along the line again, thereby restoring South Korea to it's prewar territorial status, we might all be sent to Indochina to fight the communists there. The Field Artillery medical officer seemed very amused by it all.

Later, the commander of our Heavy Weapons company came by, with the ill-disguised intent of finding out if we had any whisky available, which we didn't. I had to listen as he sat on a cot while complaining bitterly about what he called the illiterate defectives he had been getting in from the States as replacements. He noted that too many of them had nowhere near the basic reading capabilities to learn how to properly operate his outfit's weaponry.

Later, the major and I got started on writing up our experiences with field medicine techniques during Operation Ripper. Prominent were our too-frequent problems with the prompt evacuation of our wounded because of the poor roads and the adverse Korean weather. Such conditions, of course, too often ruled out the use of even the few helicopters that we otherwise would have available. We shuddered to think about how many wounded men must have died because of problems preventing timely evacuation to definitive care.

April 1st came, and we had yet to move the collecting station. I marked the day by leading the collecting station's GIs in their morning calisthenics, and appreciated that the early morning's unexpected rain shower ceased just before we started. Our line companies were patrolling in the vicinity of Sabanga-ri to the north, and meeting no enemy.

There were still no casualties coming in, and not much sick call. The regiment had just received another 300 replacements, and was now only about 200 short of being up to full strength. Most of the new men were reservists and from the National Guard, and were clearly very unhappy about being snatched away from civilian life and the jobs that they were just getting settled into so soon after World War II.

The mail finally came in that day. I received five letters and a welcomed package of canned food. Rumors were ever more plentiful about rotation, now that replacements were coming in. However, it certainly didn't look like there would be very many medical officer replacements coming in any time soon.

That evening, Intelligence reports coming in about enemy activities were highly suggestive that the enemy was in the final stages of preparing for another offensive. We also learned at 2200 that night that we were to be visited the next morning between 0900 and 1000 by not only by the visiting US Army Surgeon General, but also the

Success to Stalemate in South Korea

Far East Command (FECOM) Surgeon, the Eighth Army Surgeon, and the X Corps Surgeon. They were to be joined by our Division Surgeon who didn't visit us very often. As we scrambled about to get everything shaped up as best we could on such short notice, Bill Sloan and I took the time to try to figure out ways of entrapping our high-ranking visitors long enough to answer our questions about rotation.

By the time when all of the dignitaries were supposed to show up the following morning, our hard working personnel had succeeded in getting everything into remarkably good shape. However, the visitors' convoy of jeeps was a half-hour late. The dignitaries simply dashed round, briefly shook hands here and there, and then took off. Our division surgeon said that he did get a chance to talk to them briefly but could not get a satisfactory answer about plans for rotation. Indeed, the only information he managed to glean was that things would probably continue on as at present, at least for a while. He also made an interesting comment to the effect that in the Army, a year was considered to be the length of a tour of duty during a war in a foreign land.

I had to recognize that I needed three more months to make it to a year. Indeed, we wondered whether the whole disappointing visit was just a reaction to the torrent of letters that so many of the disgruntled medical and MSC officers had been mailing to the Army Surgeon General's office in Washington D.C.

We were still in the same place on April 4th, and while we had been told that our regiment was still officially to go into Corps reserve, plans to move us back to the south had to be delayed. Many of our deuce and a half trucks were off being used to support efforts to repair and improve roads as well as help build a bridge across the Soyang River to the north of us. Others were helping move one of our other regiments to the northeast of Chunchon and into position along that river's banks. It was to relieve a Marine regiment and clear out adjacent enemy screening units in order to secure the jump-off point for our next theater-wide offensive called "Operation Rugged."

CHAPTER 27

The next day was another quiet one, again with only a few GIs on sick call. We learned that the regiment attacking to the north of Chunchon had reached it's objectives after meeting only moderate resistance. That evening, we were told that our trucks had finally been released back to us and that we would be moving south to the vicinity of Hongchon early the following morning.

We arose at 0430 to find the area blanketed by a cold low fog. What with the final packing up and the loading of our trucks, it was 1030 before we closed in on our new positions. We had actually made relatively good time over thirty miles of much improved roads that were no longer so muddy. Our assigned bivouac area was, as so often, on the broad, sandy plain of a river valley. Several other outfits were also bivouacked near us. We were also, for the first time, able to erect the new sectional hospital ward tent we had just been issued. It was a lot like the ones used by MASH units and clearing stations.

Meanwhile, to the north, land mines were slowing our outfits advancing northwards towards the bitterly defended Hwachon Reservoir. More artillery had to be brought up for the advance to continue.

We learned the next day that an Army rotation program was finally in place and was scheduled to start on the 16th of April. However, it wasn't too clear whether medical officers would be actually getting replaced very soon. There were

Success to Stalemate in South Korea

still vacancies to be filled, as well as a number of medical officers on temporary duty still awaiting replacement.

We were also told that eligibility for rotation would be based on a point system, not just on how long a man had been in Korea. It would take 36 points in all. Men in combat line outfits accrued 4 points a month. From forward artillery positions back to regimental headquarters, it was 3 points a month. Duty anywhere else in South Korea got 2 points a month. I realized that I had already more than reached the "Points" goal. Of course, there first had to be a replacement available.

The occasional beer ration came in, and, as usual, was much appreciated, particularly since we now had something to celebrate. I dug a hole under my cot, and hid several cans of beer in it by covering it with my barracks bag.

We were also told that in three days there would be another inspection of all of our units. Meanwhile, I had the chance to check with another nearby Marine regimental medical collecting outfit, having heard that one of my medical school classmates who was a Naval medical officer was assigned there. It turned out that he had since been reassigned to one of their battalion aid stations.

The next day was spent in getting our supplies replenished and preparing for the inspection. This kept our hard-working MSC officers even busier than usual. Regimental Headquarters had even gone to the trouble of clearing brush from hills near their area. There was a sense of urgency since it was well known that our outfits on the line were meeting stiffening resistance as they continued to try to push north.

I invited the medical officer who was assigned to the Division Forward aid station for dinner. Our chief cook outdid himself by making pizza on a field range, no small feat, along with potato salad, which went very well with the beer that I had saved. It went well with our discussion of our favorite subject, which, of course, was rotation.

On the 8th, we learned that the big inspection had been postponed for two days. We wondered how long we would be staying in reserve, considering the increasing enemy pressure to the north. The Chinese were reported to again be setting grass fires so that the resultant hovering smoke would hinder aerial observation of their activities.

The next day, we had to start dealing with how to manage the rotation plan for the troops. Most of the enlisted men and officers eligible to go first were, of course, amongst our most senior and experienced people. They would be difficult to replace.

The following day, we learned that the first group to be flown to Japan for the new "Rest and Recuperation" program, better known as "R and R," or even "Rape and Run," was to be on the 12th, the day after the rescheduled inspection. My seniority relevant to rotation also made me eligible to be in that first group for the five day sojourn in Tokyo. I was actually rather loath to go, just in case, by some off-beat chance, my number might somehow come up sooner for rotation. Of course, I knew that I didn't have to worry about it, since it was far more likely that it would be many more months yet before a medical officer would be coming in to replace me.

CHAPTER 28

We finally had our inspection on the 11th of April. Everything went quite well. I then received orders to be down to the airstrip near Hoensong the following afternoon. I also got another telephone call from the MASH unit down near Hongchon that was supporting our division. It was from an old friend from medical school who was hospitalized there. I promised to drop by the next day on my way to Hoensong, since the MASH was set up beside the road to the rear that we would be using.

That night I packed up my stuff to store it while I would be away, being careful to conceal my burp gun, and tried to decide on what I wanted to shop for in Tokyo. I wanted to look for a complete set of the highly-regarded Japanese Noritake china to send home and also pick up a better little camera to replace the battered Kodak I had been using. I finally decided that I might as well take the few hundred dollars in military script I had been carrying around and send whatever I didn't spend in Tokyo to my wife via a postal money order. I arranged for a jeep and driver to take me down to the airstrip the next morning.

We left early enough for me to have the time to stop at the MASH. My friend who was hospitalized there had been suspected of having pneumonia, but it turned out to be little more than a rather bad cold, so he wasn't too sick. He had also gotten so disgusted with the regiment to which he had originally been assigned that he managed to arrange a transfer to an airborne outfit as a medical officer. As soon as he got out of the hospital he would be sent back to Japan for a few weeks of paratroop training.

At the airstrip, it was the old Army story about "hurry up and wait," but a four-engined C-54, with a full load of officers and enlisted men, finally took off for the trip across the Sea of Japan. The flight was uneventful and we landed at 1730 at Haneda Air Force Base near Tokyo. We were then taken by waiting buses to nearby Camp Drake, a large Army base, where we took off our combat clothes, showered, and were issued regular garrison–type uniforms complete with the new shorter Eisenhower jackets and appropriate rank and branch of service insignia. We had a good laugh when we watched one officer, a chaplain with one of our other regiments, choose the crossed rifle badges of an infantryman, rather than the crosses of a chaplain, to put on the lapels of his jacket. We also were able to partake of a good steak dinner.

All of this was done rather hurriedly, since time was passing by and everyone wanted to get to town before things, particularly bars, closed down. I got to talking to one of the officers in charge of our processing and learned that the whole lot of us had been re-scheduled to be bussed into nearby Yokohama rather than Tokyo as we had previously been told. However, it turned out that the officer was also from Southern California, and we got into a bit of reminiscing. The upshot of it all was that he ordered up a staff car to take me into Tokyo, and drop me off at the army-leased Yuraku hotel. It was located only about three blocks from the Dai Ichi building that was occupied by the Army Far East Command, and Eighth Army Headquarters.

As we drove into town, I was amazed at how busy the streets were. New-looking taxis, many of them American Fords and Chevrolets as well as the smaller Japanese cars, were everywhere. The people on the streets seemed to be well dressed, and the shops were brightly lit and appeared to be well supplied with merchandise. Progress through the traffic-choked streets was at times glacial. Having

Success to Stalemate in South Korea

heard the stories about all the destruction that Tokyo had suffered at the hands, or wings, of the US Army Air Force during World War II, I thought that the reconstruction accomplished during the few years since that war had ended was remarkable.

After checking in at the hotel, perhaps best described as one that might likely be patronized by business travelers, I rushed to get settled into my assigned room. Even so, it was nearly 2300 when I finally could run down the stairs to the hotel bar while hoping that it hadn't already closed. However, it was still open, and I wasted no time ordering a drink.

After a couple of sips of Scotch and water, I looked around, only to see a medical school classmate in an Army uniform standing at the other end of the bar. After rather uproarious greetings, it wasn't long until another medical officer came in who had been a year ahead of us in medical school, but was also a member of the same fraternity. It got to be a lot like old home week. After a couple more Scotches, we decided to also try some Japanese beer, which we found to be not only very good but also considerably stronger than the American variety. That we became rather snockered would be an understatement.

The next day, somewhat the worse for wear, we got together and went over to a mess in a nearby army base for breakfast. I learned that the central PX was not only sold out of Noritake china, it was also sold out of cameras, but might be restocked in a few days. This was a great disappointment, since I didn't really want to have to try to deal with the local civilian shops. Then, we took a tour by taxi of the area, soon discovering that we could go practically anywhere in Tokyo for 120 yen, then worth about 30 cents in military script.

That afternoon, I was able to place a telephone call to my wife, and got off a postal money order to her for most of the military scrip "money" I had been carrying around. Then, I put in a telephone call to a friend who had been a couple of years ahead of me in medical school and in the same fraternity. Now stationed at the Tokyo Army Hospital, he promptly invited me to dinner at the hospital officers' club that evening.

He had gone into the regular Army as a medical officer and was stationed in Japan when the Korean War broke out. He was then assigned to one of the first ill-equipped and poorly trained US Army units that were rushed from Japan to South Korea to try to help stem the sudden and overwhelming North Korean invasion in late June, 1950. When the short-lived rotation scheme for medical officers was initiated the previous February, it was prioritized by the dates of their arrival in South Korea. Being one of the first to be sent, he was one of the fortunate few that were actually rotated back to Japan.

What was now known as the Tokyo Army Hospital had reportedly been originally a large Christian civilian hospital. It was taken over by the U.S. Army at the end of World War II to care for the American army occupation troops stationed in Japan and their dependent families. The rumor was that the first thing the Army did was to remove the picture of Jesus Christ in the hospital's foyer and replace it with an even larger one of General Douglas MacArthur.

Since I arrived by taxi well before 1700, I had plenty of time to have a drink or two at the officers' club bar before dinner, which was scheduled for the comfortable time of 1830. While waiting for my host, I ordered a Scotch and water, as usual with no ice, the way I had become accustomed to drinking it, since, of course, there was little ice available for drinks in South Korea.

As I took my first sip, the friend who had invited me stepped up to the bar beside me and also ordered a drink.

He turned and said, "Having a good time?"

"You better believe it," I replied, as we shook hands. "All this is a hell of a lot better than what I've been accustomed to. Thanks a lot for inviting me."

"Oh, hell, it's good to see you. How are things at the front?"

"Well," I replied, "they're a lot better now than they were when we were down on the Pusan Perimeter."

"Christ, we had some pretty crappy times there before you guys finally arrived from the States."

I nodded. "Since Ridgway's taken over running the show in Korea from old Dug Out Doug MacArthur, everything's been going much better. Even the rations are better."

"That's what they say. Still, I'd rather be here than in South Korea."

I wondered how long he had been in the officers' club. I said, "A light day today in the operating room?"

He nodded. "I wasn't on the surgical schedule, and I'm not on call for anything tomorrow. I figured that I might as well spend my time here in the bar until dinner. My girl friend can pick me up later."

I tried to understand. I knew that after the war started, all of the wives and dependents of American army personnel who had been hurriedly sent to South Korea were soon sent back to the States, including his. He had previously also told me, when I saw him briefly in South Korea not long before he was rotated, how he had put the car he had brought over from the States during peace time up on blocks because his wife didn't have time to sell it before she was shipped out with the other dependents. But a girl friend? It was unlikely to be one of the nurses because they would have known that he had a wife.

I laughed, and said, "A musame? You?"

He shook his head. "I know what you must be thinking. When I was rotated back here last February, I was able to take my car down off the blocks and drive it. Then, I met this Japanese girl."

I nodded, although I wasn't entirely certain about what I was trying to understand. "Okay, so you were lonely."

"Not any more," he said. "She's everything I need in a woman. I didn't realize how dull things were with my wife."

I didn't want to sound like the pillar of virtue that I most definitely was not. I smiled, and said, "She must be great in bed."

For the first time, he smiled. "Boy, you better believe it. Best screwing I've ever had. Maybe it's the Asian touch."

I nodded. "But, what happens when you have to return to the States?"

He shook his head, as he put his emptied glass down on the bar. "I don't even want to think about it."

"For Christ's sake, man, you're Regular Army. They'll order you to haul ass back to the States sooner or later."

He nodded. "I know, but I'll try to postpone it a long as I can."

I couldn't help asking, "But what about your wife?"

My friend shook his head. "Damned if I know," he said. "I just know I'll never go back to that crappy little rust bucket town where we used to live. She was born there and she can have it."

After a few more drinks, it was time for dinner. My friend was getting more and more into the booze, but was by no means incoherent. While we talked about a lot of things, he clearly didn't want to go back to discussing his connubial situation.

After dinner, the bar area had become more crowded, not only with medical and MSC officers, but also off-duty nurses who enjoyed officer status. We got to talking to a group of them, and I was surprised to soon recognize one as someone I had known rather casually at a hospital in the States when I was going to medical school. She had recently joined the Army Nurse Corps and had been recently assigned to Tokyo Army Hospital.

The next day we learned that President Truman had, and as far as we were concerned very belatedly, sacked General MacArhur from being top commander of the Far East Command and promoted General Ridgeway to replace him. It didn't seem like tears were shed anywhere over MacArthur's dismissal. This was particularly true amongst the GIs and the Marines who had participated in MacArthur's ill-conceived and vainglorious invasion of North Korea, where so many of us had to suffer the catastrophic consequences of his folly.

However, while I pretty much understood the significance of it all, I was not about to let it interfere with partying, which, it must be admitted, was soon in full swing.

It is rather difficult to explain how soldiers feel during those few days of "R & R," except to those who have experienced it themselves.

CHAPTER 29

We got up early on April 18th for the processing for our return to South Korea, which meant returning to Camp Drake to turn in the garrison type uniforms and get back into our combat gear. Our bus finally left Camp Drake at 1100. At the Haneda air force base, a C-54 transport plane was loaded with GIs of all ranks returning from R&R, and we were soon on the way back to Korea. Most of them seemed well oiled and promptly went to sleep. The trip back over the Sea of Japan was uneventful, and it wasn't long until the all too familiar rugged and dun-colored mountainous terrain of South Korea, splashed here and there with early-spring green, came into view.

We landed at the very busy airstrip near Hoensong at 1530. However, we had to wait for other transport planes to land and unload their passengers. We were then all loaded onto several waiting trucks for the trip back up to Hongchon, from where we were sent back to our individual outfits. It was soon apparent that it hadn't recently rained much, judging from the thick powdery dust kicked up by the trucks as they traveled along the bone-dry dirt roads.

Regiment and the collecting station were still set up in the same places. Only one of the division's regiments was on the line. The other two, including ours, were still in reserve and training status. It was apparent immediately that the rotation program, at least for just about all GI's except for medical officers, had gotten into full swing. Since

Success to Stalemate in South Korea

our regiment was one of the first to arrive in South Korea from the States in the summer of 1950, an inordinate number of our senior and experienced non-comissioned personnel who had been near the top of the rotation list were already gone.

We initially filled the resultant personnel gaps in the collecting station with men who had been out in the battalion aid stations. With a few exceptions, the new arrivals then replaced them. Getting all of the newly arrived men trained and settled in their new assignments wasn't easy. It was almost like starting to organize the whole outfit all over again. A rumor amongst the GIs was that the reason why the regiment hadn't yet been ordered back on the line was because of the need to resolve the problem.

However, in one regiment there was probably yet another reason. It had an all-black battalion that was well regarded. Indeed, it's proud military traditions dated back to service in Civil War and on the western American frontier.

During the hectic first months of the war, all of the American outfits on the line sustained a lot of casualties. As replacements came in they were sent out to line outfits without concern for race. The previously all-black battalion soon became as nearly as racially integrated as were the other two battalions in the regiment. Of course, the entire army was supposed to have become racially integrated two years before the start of the Korean War.

An already very unpopular corps commander, a Southerner known for his racist views, now decided that the previously all black battalion should as far as possible be "disintegrated" back into an all-black status, while the other two battalions should again become all-white. While key black personnel could stay with their current units, all the rest of the black soldiers throughout the regiment were to be immediately transferred to the once all-black battalion, and as far as possible, the white soldiers in it were to be reassigned to the other two battalions.

What actually happened was that men who were regarded as "eight-balls," or the less competent and motivated GIs, both black and white, somehow wound up being reassigned to the previously all-black battalion. The other two battalions came to number only about 800 men each, where 901 were authorized, while the ranks of the third battalion swelled to nearly 1100. The results of this ill-advised program were very difficult, if inadvertently so, organizational problems. It was taking longer than expected to sort them all out.

CHAPTER 30

The Regimental Service Company officers had decided to host a cocktail party in their area on the early evening of April 19th, the day after I returned from R & R. It was to celebrate the fact that, while I was in Japan, the regimental whisky ration had at last come in. The officers of Collecting were among those invited. An unused squad tent was erected for the occasion and bars made up of packing cases and covered with GI blankets were set up at either end.

We had, in fact, what might be described as a rather pleasant event that night, with every one in reasonably clean uniforms and on their best behavior. Although it was planned to be just a cocktail party, few of us ever got around to making it to a chow line in time for dinner.

While other divisions now advancing cautiously northwards were meeting only spotty resistance, intelligence reports were coming in about another massive build-up behind the enemy's lines. The outfits to the west that were pushing into the "Iron Triangle" area reported on the 22nd that they were beginning to meet stiffening resistance. A British Brigade further to the west and just north of Seoul was reported to have suddenly become nearly surrounded by enemy but was making a brave stand.

That day we learned that 200 newly inducted medical officers were being started through four month combat medicine courses at the Medical Field Service School in Texas. It was also said that most of them were subsequently to be assigned to either Stateside medical facilities, or to military hospitals in Europe that were being expanded to support the military build-up there to block perceived Cold War threats from communist Russia. It seemed that the Far East Command, for some unknown reason and despite the hot war in Korea, had not requested their fair share of the new medical officers, or so we were told.

Rumors about marijuana smoking amongst some GIs became rampant. That night, a surprise check of one of the battalion's areas where the men slept confirmed that the rumors were largely true. We were rather surprised to learn that the GIs had figured out that the ubiquitous floor mats so widely used in Korea were woven from a kind of straw-like plant that was a close cousin of marijuana. What the GIs were doing was smoking straw torn from their mats in roll-your-own cigarette papers. However, when we officers discussed it, we had to admit that there had been no known behavioral problems as result of the mat smoking. For whatever reasons, we heard no more about the matter.

On the 23rd, the long–expected CCF "5th Phase" offensive hit the two Corps areas over to the west of us near the main north-south roads. It only minimally affected our Corps area, perhaps because we were now positioned away to the east in more mountainous country, and at some distance from those important roads.

We were not getting in many casualties while fierce battles were raging to the north and west. One of our division's regiments to the west of our positions was dealing with a serious penetration by the CCF that soon formed a dangerous salient. It was caused by an ROK Division on the regiment's flank that had collapsed under CCF pressure and "bugged out." Further over to the west, the British-led Commonwealth Division continued to be heavily engaged but was holding. The Marines were soon sent in to reduce the salient.

Amidst the increasing rumors about our regiment being soon sent up on the line, we had at least some levity. On the morning of April 25th, a cool but not unpleasant day, and as I was walking back from the mess tent with Bob Howard, a couple of two and a half ton trucks drove by along the nearby rutted dirt road that was our main supply route, heading north. The trucks were packed full of soldiers, probably replacements destined for one of the line outfits. What caught my attention was that they were all singing a song that sounded like a then-popular tune called "I'm Looking Over a Four-Leaf Clover," but the words seemed to be strikingly different.

I turned to Howard, and said, "Bob, what in hell was all that?"

Howard laughed and lit a cigarette. "That's a new song that some GI with too much time on his hands thought up."

I shook my head. "I never heard it before. The tune's familiar."

"Yeah, he just made up the words. I think it begins with 'I'm looking over a well fought over Korea that I abhor.' It's kind of funny."

After a quick look over towards the entrance to the reception squad tent to make sure that the sick call line wasn't too long, I started to load my pipe as I replied, "How does it go?"

Howard puffed on his cigarette and then said, "It's something like; "I'm looking over a well fought over Korea, that I abhor; one for the money, two for the show,

"Ridgway says, 'Stay here,' but we want to go!

"There's no use complaining, we're still remaining, to do what we came here for, Korea, Korea, and diarrhea, will make the grass grow much more."

He paused, and grinned. "There's more, but you can get the picture."

I chuckled as I put a match to my pipe. "I guess it's heart-felt enough. Irving Berlin's reputation is certainly not being seriously challenged."

CHAPTER 31

It began to drizzle the next day, April 26th, as it would, off and on, for the rest of the month. Eighth Army had begun to pull back to the No Name Line to hold there. Pressure from the Chinese and the many North Korean divisions that the Russians had reorganized and resupplied was clearly increasing.

We were now ordered to send all non-tactically important equipment to the rear. On the 28th, two battalions from our regiment moved northward to back up another of our divisions' regiments that had been pushed from positions near the No Name Line and were trying to reclaim them.

May found our collecting station still bivouacked near Hongchon. On the morning of the 1st, a brilliant Korean day, I set off in a jeep at 0730 and headed towards the division clearing station that was backing us up. It was located in Hoensong, some 30 kilometers, or 20 miles, to the south. As I drove along, I was impressed to see how well the engineer outfits had widened and improved the main dirt roads, as well as all of the bridges they had built. Unfortunately, all this activity had obliterated a lot of tiny South Korean villages that had once been huddled along the sides of the previously much narrower roads.

About two miles north of Hoensong, the fuel pump on my jeep gave out.

Fortunately, a 2 1/2 ton truck belonging to another of our division's regimental collecting stations soon came by.

Success to Stalemate in South Korea

They hooked up the jeep, and gave me a ride to Division Forward's motor pool, since they were also going that way.

I stayed to eat lunch while mechanics were working on the jeep. Realizing that I had talked a bit too long and didn't really have enough time left to go on down to the clearing station, I simply called them up on a field phone to inquire about some of our patients we had sent them.

The trip back amidst a lot more vehicular traffic was dusty almost beyond belief. It was fortunate that the nearby Corps shower unit had not moved out yet, so I was able to take a shower. Mail Call brought me a package from home with some canned Mexican food, plus another most welcome one pound can of Doniford pipe tobacco.

Again, there wasn't much sick call the next day, perhaps to some extent because morale in the regiment was almost at an all-time high despite our recent rearward adjustment of positions to the No Name Line. Major Bill Sloan was off with a scouting group from Regiment checking out another regiment's bivouac area to the north in case we might be ordered to move up there.

The army, as the rotation process continued, was becoming more and more composed of replacements that were called-up Army reservists, men from the National Guard, and draftees. The number of "regulars" left in the line outfits was said to be down to 40% or even less. While these replacements were not at all happy, in fact, often very bitter, about being called up for duty and sent off to South Korea, they ultimately did surprisingly well as soldiers, despite coming from a U.S. that was increasingly unhappy with the war.

We decided at dinner in the officers' mess one evening that we ought to stage a proper going-away party for a soon-to-be-rotated MSC officer. Because of a recent lengthy dearth of whisky rations, we would have to brew up some of what was locally called "Yalu River Water," or, more humbly, "Panther Piss."

Considerable thought went into its preparation, which, of course, depended upon what was available, usually from mess stores. Dried apricots and prunes were cut into small bits, and then put into quart bottles. Yeast and two ounces or so of precious medical alcohol were then added to each bottle, which was then topped off with orange juice. Caps punctured by ventilating holes were then put on the bottles, and it was expected that in about 48 hours the brew would ferment enough to be ready to drink.

Only then did we discover that the departing MSC officer had stashed away four bottles of whisky to celebrate his rotation. Two days later, while we were drinking his whisky at his going-away party, we ceremoniously also "tapped" the bottles of brew. It was, indeed, potent, and added significantly to the merriment. Whether all of this improved morale amongst our new replacement MSC officers was not immediately clear.

We were still near Hongchon on the 2nd of May. The weather had turned quite warm and humid. That day we heard that even the Communist Chinese Forces, the CCF, had a rotation policy in place for their medical personnel who had served for six months in the combat zone.

Only one infantry company out of our regiment's three battalions was now on the line. There was very little action by the enemy in our sector.

CHAPTER 32

Late on the afternoon on the 4th of May, and under a steady drizzle, we packed up the Collecting Station and moved up to yet another forgettable place called, we thought, Saegol. As was so often the case with our chosen bivouac areas, it was on a flat riverbed between steep hills. The road to the area had become increasingly awful as we entered the valley, and not far beyond to the north it petered out entirely. While the area had probably been fertile farming country, mercifully there were no farmers around to spread "night soil" fertilizer on the many rice paddies they had abandoned.

Since we were now so much further north, at that time of the year it didn't start getting dark until well after 2000, or 8:00 PM. Even so, the road conditions had slowed down our convoy so much that we had to really hustle to get all of our tents set up while there was still some light. The next day we changed our watches to daylight saving time.

The area was also occupied by several artillery outfits, and a searchlight unit. Their beams would be reflected off clouds at night to provide a reflected sort of artificial moonlight, a great help to GIs in outpost foxholes who were anxiously waiting and watching for stealthily approaching enemy.

On the 7th of May, things were still quiet. Patrols from the line outfits reported to not be running into any signs of the enemy. The many artillery outfits in the valley would each fire only a few rounds at a time to register their big guns on likely targets, as if to deceive the enemy as to how many of them were there. While it was becoming quite warm in the daytime, it was often still cool enough at night for us to light up our little gasoline-fired heaters.

We had few patients, virtually no sick call and no battle casualties. We did get in a Korean baby girl one evening who had had her left foot badly injured a few days previously by a bullet from a strafing airplane, almost certainly one of ours. We bandaged her up as best we could, gave her a pediatric dose of penicillin and sent her back to Clearing where they would have to decide whether her foot could be saved, which didn't seem too likely.

We had troops dug in on the high ground around the valley in good defensive positions. However, it was very difficult to evacuate casualties by hand-carried litters since the trails up to where the troops were dug in were so steep and tortuous. I spent a lot of time looking for suitable landing sites for helicopters, now that we had more of them available for evacuating badly wounded. However, I could find few areas in the narrow valley that provided enough clear space for loaded choppers to be able to take off and gain enough speed to safely climb out. The flat riverbed of the valley near the collecting station was the only really suitable place.

Late that afternoon, a GI in a line company of one of the battalions threw a hand grenade box that he mistakenly thought was empty on a warming fire, while several other GIs were huddled around it. The one forgotten grenade left in the box soon exploded, leaving one man killed and six seriously injured. When the battalion aid station medical officer called me he said he had them pretty well stabilized but that they should be evacuated as quickly as possible straight to the nearest clearing station. "Quick" certainly wouldn't be possible by litter jeep or even ambulance over the lousy roads now available to us.

I then spent a frantic half hour on the field telephone, going through a surprisingly unsympathetic chain of command as I tried to get three helicopters to come up

Success to Stalemate in South Korea

from either the nearest clearing station or the MASH down in Hoensong. When the three choppers finally reached the landing area there wasn't much light left.

The medics from the battalion aid station had to load the casualties into the helicopters' pods as quickly as possible before the light faded too much for them to be able to take off. To be on the safe side, even though it was a little dangerous, the helicopters' pilots kept the engines running and the rotors slowly turning. They didn't want to take a chance on engines balking on a restart because of their infamously weak batteries. The pilots seemed to be recent arrivals in the combat zone, and were not at all familiar with the area.

It continued to be strangely quiet along the battlefront. A blanket of haze had settled in over the valley. There was concern that the enemy was again setting off smoky grass fires to block aerial observation of their activities. Intelligence reports about enemy troop movements were consistent with preparations for another offensive. We heard that our patrols were now beginning to encounter small groups of Chinese that would quickly fade away as if to avoid contact. They were thought to probably be reconnaissance groups.

By the 10th, the smoke dissipated, and aerial observers were able to report seeing a lot of enemy activity and concentrations of troops to the north. Attempts made to dislodge these concentrations met heavy resistance. In the past, the enemy, Chinese and North Korean alike, would do their moving around at night, and stay well under cover during the daytime to avoid aerial observation. Now, they didn't seem to care. Despite the continuing lull, we knew that an attack was imminent.

On the 11th of May, we expected that we would soon begin to get in a lot more casualties. The day started out with a GI, on perimeter guard around a battalion headquarters, being mistakenly shot in his left arm early in the morning by another GI, also on guard duty, when he got up from his foxhole to relieve himself. In a way, it was demonstration of the fact that the best time to get wounded, if there was such a thing, seemed to be right around dawn when fighting often died down, and there was enough light to be readily evacuated.

We also had to deal with what we initially thought were relatively minor injuries suffered by a group of South Korean civilian laborers that had been riding on a Japanese truck that got into an accident the previous evening. The laborers were scheduled to carry supplies on A-frames strapped on their backs up to our outfits that were dug in on the hills.

Then, we heard that one of that group had died during the night. I sent a detail of three of our medics, all sergeants, over to the nearby native huts where the laborers had been sleeping to check things out.

One of the men from the detail came back to confirm that there indeed was a dead man there. I went over, and, from the looks of the corpse, had to wonder if the cause might have been cholera, which was known to still be running rampant in the civilian population. I had the medics check temperatures of the other South Koreans in the hut and they found that eight of them had low-grade fevers, although they didn't seem to be sick or to have diarrhea. Even so, we separated them from the others by putting them in a separate hut, and started them on oral antibiotics. We didn't want to take any chances on an outbreak of illness amongst those laborers, since we had begun to depend so much on them. The Chinese were said to have donkeys for such work, but we didn't.

Later, at suppertime while there was still a little light left, there was a brief firefight up on one of the hills with a North Korean patrol that caused some GI casualties, so again I had to put in an emergency call for two helicopters after a battalion surgeon had called in to request them. Then, I couldn't find out whether they had picked up the wounded and gone back to Clearing or not, since the phone lines to the company that had sustained the casualties had just gone out, and of course, the helicopters had no radios. Nearby line companies that still had their wires in didn't seem to know anything about the incident. Our 'walkie talkie" radios weren't working at all well in such hilly country.

I finally found out that one of the two helicopters had somehow managed to break it's tail rotor as it attempted a take-off. The area where the two had landed turned out to be almost too restricted for a helicopter with two loaded side pods to take off and get going fast enough to climb out, although one of the two did make it out safely. However, another chopper came in to help evacuate the remaining two wounded men. Early the next morning, a couple of mechanics with a spare tail rotor were flown in and were then able to fly the unloaded chopper back. There was some grumbling about why the Army pilots didn't seem to be quite as capable from our point of view as were the Marine pilots.

CHAPTER 33

There was no combat action on May 12th, although Regiment was sending out what they called "power patrols" from one of our battalions to help take over a rather high hill mass near Chunchon. It looked like a great place to set up an observation post since it provided wide sweeping views of the country to the north as well as to the south. However, as our patrols climbed higher, they ran into a surprisingly determined and stubborn defense by at least a battalion of Chinese that was well dug in. The patrols couldn't get anywhere near the top of the hill, took a lot of casualties, and the attack was finally called off late in the afternoon. Again we had to rely on helicopters to evacuate the wounded.

Earlier in the war, emergency requests for helicopters sometimes had to go through several levels of command. Because they didn't have radios, we were often asked for very detailed information about where the helicopter was to land. However, as the pilots became more experienced this became less of a problem, since they now would often just head for the general area and let the troops on the ground signal to them about where to land.

For some reason, this time I ran into problems with my request. I finally persuaded the Major to weigh in on the situation and get the regimental commander to simply order two helicopters to the area. We then set up a shuttle over the mountain ridges to our collecting station.

Success to Stalemate in South Korea

That night, we got very little sleep because the artillery packed around us in the valley, particularly the eight inch guns, kept up a constant barrage targeting the top of that hill to soften up the Chinese forces dug in on it. Although the concussion from the muzzle blasts rattled our tents, we weren't complaining.

In the morning, three Dutch soldiers were brought in who had gotten tangled up in a minefield. Two of them had legs that were severely damaged. We had great difficulty in placing tourniquets on them to control bleeding, and they had both already lost a lot of blood.

Then, a little Korean girl was brought in with one of her fingers nearly severed from her hand. I did my best to try to reattach it although we promptly sent her down to a clearing station. In the midst all the commotion, we never did learn exactly what had caused her injury, or how much the clearing station had been able to do for her.

That day, line outfits reported only light contact with the enemy. I had time to get permission to drive up to see what could be done to help the aid station of our battalion that was involved in the so far unsuccessful attempt to take the hill. It was gratifying so see how well they were managing.

All of the line outfits were working furiously to improve their defenses, since there was no doubt that the Chinese and the North Koreans would soon be hitting us with considerable force. As a matter of fact, we were even digging foxholes around the collecting station.

On the next day, the 14th, it started to rain. This significantly hampered using helicopters, since they were still not equipped to fly in inclement weather. Two GIs had been seriously injured when a booby trap they were setting blew up prematurely. We had a very difficult time getting them down off the mountain and onto a litter jeep. One GI died while the jeep was on the way to the collecting station.

In another action, one of our medics assigned to a battalion aid station, and out with one of the line companies, was killed while on one of those Power Patrols while bandaging up a wounded soldier. The litter jeep brought in not only his body, but also what gear he had been carrying. When there were no Graves Registration outfits working nearby, we often had to check out a dead man's belongings and what he had in his pockets before sending the body to the rear. The often involved looking for anything of a demeaning sort, like porn pictures and magazines.

No one, even in the line company to which this dead man had been very recently assigned, seemed to know much about him. He had apparently kept pretty much to himself. We discovered that he had been carrying a lot of documents. They showed that he had relatively recently enlisted in the US Army. An American citizen for only two years, he came to the US from his native Greece in 1947. He had previously spent time in a fascist concentration camp during the recent civil war there, and later had fought against the communist guerillas then besieging the country. He apparently had also written a lot of poetry, and had taken over the sponsorship of an elementary school in his hometown in Greece.

I very much regretted that I had not had the opportunity to know him. Perhaps he carried a burning desire to fight the communists to his grave.

That night we treated several casualties from the day's patrols. After that, it was decided that we had to do something about providing a suitable mixer for the 190 proof medical alcohol, of which we had more than usual, to fill the vacuum until the next whisky ration was to come in. No one seemed much interested in taking the trouble to make up another batch of "Yalu River Water." We were also out of grapefruit juice, or anything else like it, to use as a mixer.

One of the dentists had the idea of using fruit-flavored Life Savers, little donut shaped candies that were supposed to sweeten one's breath. We dumped two packs of them into a canteen cup, added a half-inch or so of water, and heated the mixture over one of the little heaters until all the Life Savers had dissolved. We decided to put about a quarter of an inch of medical alcohol into some emptied

Success to Stalemate in South Korea

cheese glasses that we had gotten in packages from home, then added a half inch of the syrupy mixture, topping it off with water. In fact, the drink didn't taste badly at all, although, as it turned out, we were to have little chance to enjoy the concoction.

Later that night, our fears of another Chinese offensive became reality. It was raining heavily. The enemy first hit an ROK division over to the right of our regiment's positions. The regimental S-2 officer told me that there could be as many as four Chinese armies of three or four divisions each, along with an unknown-sized force of North Koreans, threatening us. He was now sure that they were starting out by trying to knock out that ROK division so they could get around to our rear, just as we had feared. It had been earlier thought, however, that they were more likely to focus their efforts more to our left, towards the central part of the front, where more ROK divisions were positioned.

Cautiously, our division's line outfits were shifted to the right, or east, to deny our flank to the enemy after the ROK division there not unexpectedly finally began to break up under severe pressure. One of our division's regiments, further to our right, also bore the brunt of the Chinese onslaught, and was badly clobbered. Two of their battalions were said to have lost most of their vehicles. One of their battalion medical officers was missing in action, and another was wounded. A battalion of that regiment was hit so hard that its headquarters was overrun, and it sustained so many casualties amongst it's officers that a captain was at one time acting as battalion commander. The French and Dutch battalions, also in the area, were pushed back, but later regained their ground. Despite the rain, we were again digging foxholes around the collecting station.

However, despite the fury of the enemy attacks, our line outfits, supported by the massive amount of artillery that fortunately had again been brought up, soon managed to inflict almost incredibly heavy casualties on the enemy. Support from low-flying B-26 aircraft was of major help.

We were getting surprisingly few casualties from our battalion aid stations, but we were seeing a lot from the other regiments. The artillery never seemed to pause much while firing their guns. The longest interval between muzzle blasts that I could time was only 5 seconds.

The next night, the collecting station was pulled back, a move made more complicated by the fact that we had to temporarily divide it into two units, one to leapfrog the other, because we were still busy with casualties. On the 19th, we moved even further back towards Hongchon, and into an area just recently vacated by Division Forward when it had hurriedly pulled back to the south.

While we now had surprisingly few battle casualties to deal with, a lot of prisoners were being brought in. The battalion aid stations as usual checked out many of them, but others were brought straight to our collecting station. They all seemed well fed and healthy, almost all in their early 20s, had good clothing, and sturdy shoes with thick rubber soles and canvas tops. Our new Motor Pool officer rather somberly commented that it looked like it was the more seasoned and experienced enemy soldiers that were now being captured and killed, which, he thought, might be a good thing.

The tales that were being told about the preceding battles were amazing. One machine gunner was said to have caught a group of Chinese fleeing down a hill to escape strafing aircraft, and it was figured that he "got" at least 200 of them before his gun barrel burned out. Others told of seeing groups of 200 to 300 Chinese at a time disappearing into blazing hells of napalm dropped by aircraft. There were even stories about piles of dead Chinese stacked so high that snipers were able to take cover behind them. More rumors, perhaps.

CHAPTER 34

On the 22nd of May, the collecting station of an airborne regiment went into position about two kilometers back down the dirt road that was our main supply route. The regiment was to join ours in trying to cut off and round up the estimated as many as 30,000 or so enemy left behind as their outfits were slowly beginning to retreat. Already, some of our line outfits had been able to cautiously move forward while meeting lessening resistance, so it seemed to be a good time for a counter-attack.

My two medical school classmates who had transferred to that airborne division had just joined it after completing their paratrooper training in Japan. It was nearly inevitable that we would get together when we had the chance. We did so that evening while things were relatively quiet.

We ate dinner at our mess, and then watched a motion picture about auto racing starring Clark Gable while sipping from a bottle of "refreshment" that they had brought with them. My friends said that four of the medical officers in their regiment had already been rotated, despite the fact that the airborne outfit had arrived in South Korea well after most of our outfits.

We then repaired to my tent, and, in due time we started singing some of the old songs. This did not appeal very much to the assistant regimental commander, the S-5, also known to the troops as "Iron Ass," who phoned over twice from his nearby tent to tell us to "shut the hell up." After the second call, I realized I had better close down the party and send the two of them off while at least one of them could still drive their jeep.

As they drove off, they were singing a rather sardonic song that must have dated back at least to the British in World War I. It started out with "The bells of hell go ting-a-ling-a-ling for you but not for me." The last line, floating out over the nearby rice paddies as their departing jeep noisily sloshed through the mud, went, "The bells of hell go ting-a-ling-a-ling for you but not for me, so blow it out your ass." That last, most probably, was a Yank improvisation.

The next day, our collecting station was ordered to move forward to keep up with our advancing troops, and to bivouac in much the same area we had occupied during the last days of March and early April. As has been noted, this back and forth sort of movement did not cause any concern, since General Ridgway had repeatedly insisted that our goal was not so much fighting for territory, but rather to eliminate as many communist soldiers as possible.

We weren't at all busy, so while we were waiting to move out, I thought that I would have time before we would move out to drive over to the nearby Navy medical unit that was supporting a Marine regiment. There, I was able to catch up with another classmate of mine. When I drove back, I realized I had cut the time a bit too close when I saw the last serial of our collecting station convoy of vehicles again heading north. At the same time, units of our division had jumped off in an attack to the north along with the airborne outfit as planned. A bridgehead was soon secured on the Soyang River. Our regiment was at last becoming heavily involved.

Along with the casualties, great numbers of Chinese prisoners were still being captured. It was said that they were now surrendering at a rate of 50 to 75 a day. Apparently they were all near starving, having been on very short rations as the result of American air strikes disrupting their long supply lines from the north. By the 25th, patrols were encountering few organized enemy groups.

The next day, since our regiment was slated to go into Corps reserve, the collecting station moved back to the vicinity of Hangye. Bill Sloan had just departed to the States, and had been replaced by a recently arrived medical officer, also a major. The Navy doctor, Henry Marshall, that had been assigned to one of our battalions had finally been rotated, so I went up to their aid station near Inje to temporarily hold the fort until his long-expected and now well overdue replacement showed up. We had heard that about 150 medical officer replacements would be coming in within the next two weeks.

The battalion's line companies were dug in across a valley protecting the bridgehead on the river just beyond it. This battalion, also to go into reserve with the regiment, had taken the place of the French battalion that, quickly reorganized with replacements, had been sent further north. It was raining heavily again, but it wasn't too cold.

The numbers of Chinese surrendering seemed to be ever increasing. The troops hit on a good idea. Whenever a Chinese surrendered, they would give him a box of C-rations and let him go. As often as not, he would return with many of his comrades. In one instance, it was reported, or perhaps rumored if perhaps somewhat inaccurately, that one Chinese soldier so treated somehow managed bring back nearly 1500 of his comrades. The Chinese supply line from so far to the north was most likely becoming ever more compromised, since the clearing weather permitted an increasing frequency of American air strikes. Much the same problem had been a major factor in the defeat of the invading North Korean Peoples Army, the In Mun Gun, seven months earlier. Nonetheless, the enemy now seemed to have somehow succeeded in bringing in more artillery.

I was saddened to learn that the younger of the two brothers who were medics in the Red battalion's aid station had been killed. He had already been transferred back to the aid station from his previous assignment as a rifle company medic and promoted to sergeant. The battalion's troops had been advancing across some very hilly country and meeting only light opposition from small groups of enemy.

Apparently, the aid station had received a call about some wounded men having taken refuge in a ravine in nearby hills. The two brothers climbed into a litter jeep with their field medical kits to go help. However, when they arrived at the site mentioned, they found no sign of any wounded men. Believing it had all been a false alarm, they turned and went back down the hill. The younger brother suddenly fell, having been shot through the chest by a sniper and died almost instantly in his older brother's arms.

The rains continued, and the river rose over three feet. This again played hell with our transportation. The bridge was nearly washed out, and while trying to cross the flooding river, a Marine truck turned over, and later, a tank's engine was drowned out. The regiments on the attack soon had to pause while they received an airdrop of supplies. Fortunately, the weather soon cleared again. The Marines brought up two of their amphibious 2 1/2 ton trucks originally designed to support assault landings. We also had some of the engineer's boats to use.

As the month of May waned, the regimental whisky ration as well as the beer ration finally came in. We were also issued division shoulder patches to sew onto the left upper sleeves of our herringbone cotton twill shirts and field jackets. Such insignia hadn't been worn by the combat line troops since very early in the war. We had, of course, at regimental level, already gone back to wearing insignia of rank and branch of service on the outsides of our collars. Things had certainly changed since those frantic and helter-skelter days earlier in the war when we were desperately trying to defend the Pusan Perimeter from the menacing North Korean army.

CHAPTER 35

On the 1st of June, the battalion headquarters and the medical aid station moved a few miles to the north. The rain-swollen rivers were now more easily crossed thanks to the efforts of the engineer battalions to build and repair bridges. Our regiment had been ordered to replace another regiment and then capture another high hill to the north. It was thought that this would take only a few days, after which the regiment would pull back to join the rest of the division in Army reserve.

We were now positioned right on the 38th Parallel and in the more mountainous country towards the eastern side of the Korean peninsula. We knew that there had been plans for mopping-up operations to round up fleeing enemy. However, it had become all too apparent that there were a lot of pockets of Chinese and North Koreans that had been bypassed and were stubbornly holding out. They would have to be eliminated before broader operations could be effectively initiated.

On the morning of the 3rd, the battalion moved north to an area about four miles, or seven kilometers, beyond the ruined town of Inje. It was a rather pretty morning. The road meandered along beneath steep bluffs overlooking a river valley. Rusting remains of burned out vehicles peeked out from behind the abundant foliage of weeds along the sides of the road.

However, we could not immediately take our vehicles all the way. A section of the narrow road was now only a wide and rather deep ditch due to North Korean infiltrators blowing up a culvert that ran under it. This meant that those of us in the battalion medical aid station had to walk behind the line companies for the time being and work out of our field medical kits. Combat engineers feverishly working on the damaged section of the road told us that we should be able to bring up at least some of our wheeled vehicles by mid-afternoon.

We then came to the pontoon bridge across the river that was on the way to the jump-off point for the attack. There was a good view of the high hill that was the regiment's objective. An observation post on top of it would dominate the escape corridors of any enemy that had been left behind.

After walking across the bridge, we soon came up to the positions of the outfits that we were to replace. Their attempts to capture the high ground on the hill had all been relentlessly beaten back. Rounds were coming in ahead of us from mortars and what sounded like from 105 mm howitzers, possibly some of ours that had been captured by the enemy, if not armament of their own they had recently managed to bring in.

Shortly after a couple of our litter jeeps were able to catch up with us on the hastily repaired road, we received our first casualty. It was an infantry captain who had sustained a severe abdominal wound while leading one of the line companies that had marched in ahead of us.

When our 3/4 ton truck finally arrived, we parked it off to the side of the road and worked out of the back of it. It started to rain, although not heavily. Evacuating casualties down the narrow road was somewhat complicated by the other regiment's troops as they straggled back though our positions while they moved to the rear. The narrow road soon became jammed with to and fro traffic.

The North Koreans dug in on the hill proved to be tenacious fighters. The battalion that was leading the attack soon suffered over 70 casualties, and the battalion

I was temporarily with had 36 of them by nightfall. Very little ground had been gained.

We closed in as tightly as we dared that night. Dinner was from C-rations. It proved to be noisy. Mercifully, the rain had stopped. We spent the night on opened litters on the ground beside the truck while we listened to our artillery. Besides thunderously pounding the hill, they were also sending shells over the river to harass places the forward observers had spotted where the enemy might be gathering their forces during the night.

We set up our aid station tent the next morning. The only patients we saw were those on sick call. Cautious patrols hoping to encircle and capture North Koreans up on the hill discovered that they had abandoned their positions during the night. Perhaps the incessant artillery barrage had driven them away. Only one of our battalions had any real trouble, when they ran into yet another pocket of rather obstinate North Koreans.

Once the road was reported to be completely cleared of mines, we struck the aid station tent and drove farther north, into a wild and beautiful gorge. It was bordered on both sides by precipitous rough-hewn and scarred bluffs with shreds of haze still clinging to higher ground. The area had an undeniably Oriental look to it, something like a stylized Chinese landscape painting.

Again, we ran into another section of road that had been destroyed. So, we turned our vehicles around and returned to the nearest abandoned rice paddy near the tents of the battalion command post. Just as we were unloading our CP tent, the rain started again, soon turning the ground into a muddy mess. We were all thoroughly soaked by the time we got the tent erected.

The night turned out to be reasonably peaceful. The only incoming rounds were landing several hundred yards away. The battalion headquarters mess, still well in the rear, sent up a very good steak dinner in Marmite containers. We now had no casualties to deal with. Our line companies were having trouble in the rain and the dark finding their designated positions in the mountainous terrain bordering

John Benton

the valley where they were supposed to dig in. Fortunately, their only opposition was the weather.

CHAPTER 36

The rain continued, and June 4th dawned dreary and dull. The line outfits were all finally dug in on their assigned positions. The only gunfire we heard was off to the west, which meant that the battalion over there, unlike the rest of the regiment, had run into some enemy, although it all died out shortly after noon. That night was also quiet, and the rain finally started to taper off.

The next day was overcast with only occasional rain showers. We were still not receiving any battle casualties, and seeing just the more or less usual sick call. Now, we were told that we would finally be moving to the rear to go into reserve near Inje, but the road, little more than single lane, was now jammed by ROK units moving northwards in their heavily loaded Japanese trucks. We finally were able to move back when the road cleared and, as we had expected, returned to a bivouac area in the vicinity of the regimental area near Inje. By the 8th, we were well settled in.

We were concerned about why the replacement for the rotated Naval medical officer still had not shown up. The battalion aid station MSC officer and I decided that, since things were so quiet, we would drive down to Division Rear and check with the division surgeon's office and try to find out when we could reasonably expect said replacement to arrive. With me still filling in at the battalion aid station, the newly-arrived major replacing Sloan was getting a little tired of having to do all of Collecting's doctoring by himself.

After the skies cleared, the roads soon dried out and became very dusty again. In that area, the heavily traveled road was well maintained by several engineer battalions. The bridge across the Pukhan River now even had what looked like cloverleaf approaches. The trip, some 30 miles by way of Hangye, took us nearly three hours because of the heavy stop-and-go traffic.

The division medical officer was able to confirm that some medical officer replacements were indeed coming in. However, they still needed a few more of them to fill the vacancies that would be left after the last of the temporary duty Army medical officers had departed.

As we started on the return trip, the traffic being what it was, we realized that we would probably not make it back to the battalion in time for chow. So, we stopped at Division Forward. As usual, they were quite hospitable. The MSC officer already knew many of his counterparts there.

Capt. MacDonald was also there, since his ambulance unit was still based nearby. While we were enjoying a welcomed beer while waiting for dinner, he related a very disturbing story to us. Since he got around so much in the whole Division area while supervising his ambulances, he always seemed to be tuned in to the latest rumors.

This one was about something that supposedly had happened out in the once all-black battalion, the one that had been nearly destroyed by misguided, racist, and ultimately unsuccessful high-command attempts to reverse the integration of its personnel and return it to an all-black soldier outfit.

It was common knowledge that the battalion's officers and non-coms had nearly reached their wits' end while trying figure out what to do with so many of the near-useless GIs, both black and white, that had been dumped into their battalion's ranks. Too many were the kind of soldiers who were inclined to "bug out" at even the whisper of a chance of a combat action, probably the main reason why they had been transferred from other units in the first place.

The once-proud battalion had become reduced to being considered untrustworthy. Indeed, things had gotten so bad that, according to the rumor, that on more than one occasion, medical corpsmen out with the battalion's infantry companies had to use their carbines to shoot at the heels of the reluctant soldiers they were following when on the attack, just to keep them advancing and not bugging out.

One morning, the unfortunate battalion, not trusted at that point to do much of anything, was simply holding some ground and taking no enemy fire at all. The other two battalions of that regiment were on the attack at some distance, one or two kilometers, in front of it. At daylight, the corpses of twelve GIs that had apparently been shot at close range were found along the side of a road in the battalion's area. All of them were said to be chronic AWOLs and eight-balls. Nobody professed to know anything about what had happened, or if they did, they probably wouldn't have admitted to it. Of course, suspicions were rife.

I asked Mac if he thought the story was for real, although even wilder rumors had been circulated in the past. He shook his head, and said that while he hadn't been over in that regiment's sector recently, he had heard the rumor back at Division's motor pool a week or so previously when he was picking up an ambulance that had been repaired. And, as a matter of fact, I never heard anything more about it either, even if the rumor was for real.

The MSC officer in the battalion aid station where I was temporarily assigned later told me that he had heard the same story, although he hadn't taken much stock in it. However, I had also heard that that battalion had recently, and rather suddenly, become a great deal more combat effective. One can only guess at a possible correlation, if indeed there ever was one.

There were still a lot of problems with supplying our more forward units by using wheeled vehicles. Later in the day, we learned that there would be an airdrop of supplies for those units. Usually, C-119 aircraft were used.

John Benton

Towards evening, after we had returned to the battalion area and while there was still some light, the artillery all around us got to work as their forward observers tried to visually register their guns on potential gathering places of the enemy during the coming night. Soon, over the muzzle blasts of the artillery, we heard the sound of aircraft engines, as the three expected C-119 cargo planes in formation passed overhead towards the north. The rain that so often came with the setting of the sun hadn't yet started. We could see the planes circling in the distance as they tried to identify their drop zones.

Just as the lead plane let go several pallets carrying supplies under their colorful parachutes, a battery of 155 mm. howitzers near us suddenly opened up, probably on a time-on-target shoot, where a specific target had been picked, and a time set for bombarding it. Instantly, we realized that there must have been a serious lack of communication somewhere. The ill-fated planes flew right into the path of the shells, were all hit, one after the other, and after exploding, dived down to fiery crashes, as supplies and their parachutes that fell out behind them mixed in with black, greasy smoke. Then, it began to rain.

CHAPTER 37

The next day, the 9th of June, was partly cloudy with some sunshine and towards evening occasional rain showers. We were again undergoing re-supply and training of the new replacements that were still coming in to replace those being rotated. There were few casualties to treat, just sick call, which meant dealing with sprains and occasional fractures, and the other usual ailments, such as rashes, abrasions, upset stomachs, sore backs and feet, colds, diarrhea, and the like.

I tried to teach our medics how to deal with such matters on their own to improve their capabilities in the field, and how to recognize when a more serious problem was present that merited the prompt attention of a medical officer. This was possible because we were dealing mostly with young, healthy males who tended to have rather simple and uncomplicated medical problems.

The war was clearly becoming stabilized. Mail service continued to improve. Packages from home were regularly arriving from the States. Indeed, it now took the mail just seven to ten days to come in from the States.

Even the beer and whisky rations were coming through more regularly. This facilitated our hosting occasional get-togethers with officers from the military forces of other countries serving near us who were operating under the flag of the United Nations. Of course, we were all pretty much in our twenties and early thirties. Discussions were often fascinating, particularly when getting the viewpoints about what was happening from officers from the other countries.

The percentage of "regular" Army men continued to drop as draftees, called- up reservists and National Guardsmen were sent to us as replacements, not only for combat casualties but also for men being rotated. While these men had often received considerable medical aid training in the States, they still had much to learn about the unique situations they would be facing in South Korea.

Our bivouac areas when we were in reserve status were, of course, much neater and better organized than when we were on the line. For the battalion, now bivouacked near Regiment, it was almost like being in garrison status.

We continued to have movies nearly every night after it grew dark, around 2100, in the shell of a shot-up and roofless building that some GIs thought, for whatever reason, had once been occupied by Russian advisors to the NKPA. When it rained, a tent would be found.

The shows, still using 16 millimeter sound film, were always well attended. Many of the movies continued, of course, to be the "B" pictures that the Hollywood studios were grinding out for the popular double feature movie theater shows. However, some of the films were first rate. They were all very well received by our homesick GIs. Marines and ROK soldiers that were bivouacked nearby often joined us in our somewhat impromptu outdoor movie theater.

The first clear night for a long time, and a beautiful one at that, was on the 12th. I sat through one reel of the movie and left, it was such a turkey, which didn't seem to bother most of the other viewers. A party soon shaped up in Collecting's otherwise idle reception tent, with several officers from Regiment Headquarters as well as the service company bringing in bottles. We really had the best set-up for parties, that is, on the rare occasions when we were not seeing patients.

The good weather held only until the afternoon of the 15th. A thunderstorm suddenly roared in and turned the ground back into gooey mud. As I stood by the tent entrance, while loading my pipe and watching the downpour, I said to Honsho, now the "Number One" aid station houseboy, "Toksan (a lot) rain."

He nodded as he grinned and replied, "many, many."

"Many next month?"

"Toksan more. Many, many more!"

Honsho, whose real name was Kim Hong Bea, was putting the finishing touches on a sort of scarf to be worn as an Ascot cravat with our open collared cotton twill shirts. Men in Army units in rear areas were now often wearing them in colors appropriate to their units. For the infantry, the color was blue. Honcho was cutting one out from a piece of blue nylon material from a parachute that had been used for an aerial supply drop. Such may have been somewhat illegal, but there were a lot of such parachutes scattered around because of the frequency of supply drops. We could also use the material from the red parachutes that identified drums of gasoline, since it's color was, not unexpectedly, close to the official color of the Medical Corps.

I was still, and with some degree of desperation, mulling over an event that had occurred that morning. I was awakened by gunshots that were clearly from an M1 rifle, and were coming in our direction. I climbed out of my sleeping bag, hastily put on my boots and grabbed my .45 automatic.

It was not long after first light. Outside the tent, one of our medical techs was standing and intently peering up the adjacent hillside.

Lt. Armstrong, the MSC officer who had replaced Hayes, also standing near the tent, said, "Christ, Sergeant, what the fuck's happening?"

The sergeant shook his head. "Damned if I know, sir, but some asshole up on that hill is shooting down into this area. I don't think it's a gook because it sounds like an M1 that he's firing. Thank God he hasn't hit anything yet."

"Does this happen around here very often?" I said anxiously, as I cocked the .45 and slipped off the safety catch.

Armstrong shook his head as he stared up the low hill. "Whoever's up there must have already used up a whole ammo clip. He's got to be reloading."

Then, a group of GIs with their M1 rifles at the ready ran by on the double and started to spread out to flank whoever was doing the shooting. I also recognized one of our aid men following the detachment.

Major Hirsch, the battalion CO, came running toward us. He was clearly upset. "That's got to be that son of a bitch Ollie Winters sure as hell!"

I shook my head. "Do you mean to tell me that the crazy little bastard is still around? Christ, how many times has he been evacuated as a psycho?"

"Those rear echelon assholes keep sending him back," said Hirsch. "He usually straightens out for awhile, but then he seems to go off his rocker again. I sure got an ear full about him from his company CO just before he was rotated."

"I can't understand why in hell they keep sending him back," I said. Of course, I well remembered him telling me how he wanted to be transferred out of a line outfit because he wanted to survive so he could take care of his ill mother.

Armstrong lit a cigarette. "Maybe his personnel records are all fucked up because of all the times he's been evacuated."

It wasn't long before Ollie was brought down from the hill with his hands high in the air, while he was shepherded by the other members of his company that had gone up the hillside to get him. From the expressions on their faces, it was a wonder that he hadn't wound up dead.

He was picked up by two MPs, handcuffed, and taken under guard back to Division Rear to undoubtedly face severe military justice. It wasn't an hour until the field telephone in the aid station rang. On the line was a Red Cross representative wanting to know where Ollie had been sent. They had just gotten an urgent message to inform him that his mother had died.

We never saw Ollie again.

CHAPTER 38

As June wore on, we became even more involved with the ongoing training of our mostly none-to-happy replacements. There were still only a few combat casualties to deal with, although there were accident victims to treat, and of course, the daily routine of sick call.

Shower units, set up near fast-flowing creeks or streams, were now much more commonly available, so we became a much neater-looking lot. The GIs in the line companies no longer resembled the ragamuffin types that had been typical for so long, probably because the much warmer weather meant that they didn't have to wear all the layers of clothing they did during the winter. Now, they only wore their green cotton twill field trousers and shirt-jackets. They also had access to brother GIs who had barbering skills and would provide haircuts, hopefully for tips.

And then there was the matter of my new boots. All along we had worn the standard Army boots that dated back to early in World War II, give or take the Shoepacs we had worn during the recent winter. We were still blousing our trousers over the boots by tucking the bottom ends of them up under rubber bands, or condoms, between the two straps on the sides of the cuffs.

One of the regimental chaplains, who was seriously considering leaving his church to join another, was still waiting to hear whether the Army would accept the change. Somewhat to his surprise, he was issued pair of the new style infantry boots, apparently because he was a chaplain. It would have likely been a long time before such boots would be generally issued to the GIs in the infantry line companies. They were notably different from our existing standard issue ones in that they were made of shiny leather and were laced all the way to the top. Indeed, they were very much like paratrooper boots.

The chaplain was scheduled to go on R & R to Japan, and he had decided that while he wanted to see what real life was all about, he also wanted to avoid any disease issues in the process. It seems that he had a sort of girl friend back in the States and had finally decided that he wanted her to become a "real" girlfriend in every sense of the word, even if it meant leaving his church with it's vows of celibacy. He offered me a deal. So, a bottle of 100 Aureomycin capsules changed hands, as did the boots. They were a bit wide for my feet, but wearing two pairs of GI issue socks at a time took care of the problem.

The 20th of June was a bit more eventful. Without warning, as was always the case, people from Division came around again to collect all of our military script and exchange it for a new issue. It hadn't been long since a previous surprise change, but they did it in an irregular way because it helped to prevent counterfeiting. I decided to go down to the army post office at Division Forward and convert the $223 I was carrying into a postal money order made out to myself that I could always cash in, and save myself some of the trouble associated with any more script changes.

The new division surgeon visited us that afternoon. His uniform was almost painfully new, as compared to our rather faded outfits. It turned out that he had been a member of the same medical school fraternity that I did, although at a different university. Neither one of us could remember the fraternity's secret handshake. He said that a few new medical officer replacements would be coming in soon, but as far as he knew there would be still only be enough of them to replace the last of the Army docs on TDY.

Success to Stalemate in South Korea

Anyhow, the visit served as a good excuse for a little party, as if we really needed one. A spare squad tent was set up in Collecting's area, and all the officers in the regiment were invited. Even more actually showed up. They were all soon into singing the bawdy old favorites, such as, "Behind Those Swinging Doors," "Salvation is Free ('throw a nickel on the drum, save another drunken bum')," "Minnie the Mermaid," and "O'Reilly's Daughter." Of course, the new division surgeon and I had to do the official song of our fraternity, inelegantly known as "The Rupture Song," which began with "Oopsie doodle, I'm off my noodle, I'm tired of wearing a truss, my rupture's gone..."

I was pouring myself one last drink when the division surgeon, who could be only a few years older than I was, came by. By this time we had chatted a few times during the afternoon. With a canteen cup of Scotch in hand, he said, "I'm still kind of curious about how you managed to escape from that fucked up disaster in North Korea."

I could almost laugh about it now. "It sure wasn't easy."

"I'll bet," he said. "I also heard that you were a battalion surgeon in one of our regiments that was shot up the most when the Chinese army suddenly came into the war, and then you were all ambushed by a Chinese division when you tried to retreat."

"That's right."

He lit a cigarette, as he shook his head and said, "How the hell did you manage to get out?"

"Well," I said after a moment, "for on thing, I was riding in a serial of vehicles that was near the front of the column as we tried to drive through the roadblock. Some of the Chinese were probably still setting up their weapons. We seemed to have been a lot luckier than the outfits behind us."

"I also heard that you had to walk out."

I decided to light my pipe, and fished it out of a pocket, along with my tobacco pouch. "That was after both our trucks broke down. We didn't have a hell of a lot of choice. After we got a tank to tow out the truck with our litter cases, we got the walking wounded down off the other truck. We were able to sneak through the Chinese positions and work our way south through the hills."

"That's where you really got lucky," he said, as he lit another cigarette.

"Was it ever," I said, as I lit my pipe. "It was just one huge, unbelievably fucked-up chaotic bug-out. The whole command structure fell apart. It was every man for himself."

"How many men did your outfit loose?"

I paused before replying. "Christ, when we got down to Sunchon where we were supposed to regroup, we only had maybe 80 left out of the original 200 in our regimental collecting company, which included the three battalion aid stations. Of course, we'd already lost a lot of people even before we hit that damned roadblock. In my aid station, we had ten left of the original 28."

He shook his head. "We sure don't train our people for that kind of shit."

"Well, most of our people that did make it out were from our supply and mess outfits that were sent out the previous day. They used a road over to the west. The Chinese hadn't gotten over that far."

"Why didn't you guys go out that way?"

I shook my head. "Oh, we were told that if we tried to use that road, it would screw everything up because it was being used for the evacuation of all the rest of the Eighth Army outfits northwest of there. So, in a way, we wound up holding the gate against the whole damned Chinese army."

"While the rest bugged out?"

I had to laugh, if rather grimly. "Yeah, sort of like that."

"I'm sure as hell no military tactician, but couldn't you guys go out in combat formation, with the infantry running along up on the hills to take out the Chinese?"

"Oh, Christ," I replied, "everybody that was still alive had been up night and day for over a week while we tried to retreat after they first hit us. Everybody was on benzedrine just to keep going. We didn't have a single rifle company left that was capable of running those ridges. I guess the brass just decided that, shot up as we were, about all we could do was to load up in what few vehicles we had left and make a run for it."

"Yeah, I heard about that, and how your people were able to warn the Marines and the army division on the other side of the peninsula about the Chinese coming into the war."

I smiled, and said, "Well, it gave them a few days' grace to organize what they called their "attack to the rear."

"Right," he said, finishing the drink. "They sure had their problems, too."

After it began to get dark, which was about 2130, we all went to the near-nightly motion picture show. Entitled "Go For Broke," the movie was a good one about the battalion of Japanese–American soldiers that fought in Italy during World War II and had been so heavily decorated for bravery. I could not help but recall that so many of those men, most of them born in the US, had been among the West Coast Japanese that were rounded up early in that war and put in detention camps.

The next day was hot and humid. We began to prepare for what we decided would be just about the biggest party ever thrown by the military in South Korea. The occasion was the regimental commander being rotated back to the States. Three squad tents were set up side by side near an adjacent airstrip. The regimental CO commented that signs should be posted to warn incoming aircraft to "Watch out for low flying personnel."

When Honsho brought me my washed spare field uniform, I decided to ask him to help me shine my boots. Even the standard ones that had the rough side of the leather on the outside like suede could be shined, if enough polish was used. Honsho had become quite expert at it. I didn't think it prudent to wear my new boots in public just yet.

He nodded, and picked up the little can of shoe polish and a rag he had saved. As he started to put polish on the boots, he asked, "Show tonight?"

His English was getting much better than my Korean. I nodded, and replied, "Samo, samo."

He shook his head. "People talk, I don' know. Me looky, looky at movie, then me know."

Every day he would ask, "Chungook cutta-cutta?" which translated into, "Are the Chinese pulling out?"

He had lived in Manchuria for eight years, and had nothing good to say about the Russians he had encountered there. He had returned to his native Seoul just after the war in the Pacific ended to go into business.

A couple of days previously, I was trying to explain the Japanese reaction to the Korean War without apparent success. I decided to try again by describing, as best I could, how they were beefing up their police forces to becoming a defensive force more like soldiers, and that the Americans were helping them to do so. I said, "Japanese talking about have-a-yes policemen to fight communists."

"Oh no!" Honsho exclaimed as he puffed on his pipe. "No good Japanese have soldiers, poricemen have-a-yes."

"Samo-samo policemen," I said. "Even have scoshi artillery."

Hosho looked puzzled. "Artirrery?"

"Boom-boom. Toksan boom-boom."

His face lit up, as he said, "Ah, so! Poricemen?"

"Policemen yes," I continued, "not like soldiers but have jeep-os, tank-os. Maybe some day make army samo-samo GIs."

Honsho's round face clouded. "No fucking good," he muttered. "Japanese no fucking good. No good for Korea mens."

"Japanese army 1945, Japanese now, no samo-samo," I replied, well understanding that the Japanese occupation of Korea for four decades from the early 1900s to the end of World War II had left most South Koreans thoroughly mad at them. I said, "New Japanese be samo-samo United Nations men." I wasn't quite sure he understood.

"Mebbe so, I don' know," said Honsho, again dubiously shaking his head. It was clear that he totally disapproved of the Japanese having a standing army again, even if it wasn't what I was trying to tell him.

While we were talking, he had done an excellent job of shining the boots. I slipped him some military script. As the Number One of all our regimental medical company houseboys, he was their leader, perhaps because he was a bit older and spoke at least a little English.

CHAPTER 39

The party on June 21st was, by all accounts, a howling success, in more ways than one. Since things were very quiet, almost all of the battalion and regimental officers were there. Many Division officers also showed up, as well as guests from other outfits.

Two bars were set up, with favored sergeants doing the pouring. The average consumption of whisky estimate was later said to be nearly a half a fifth per man, although that figure must have been greatly exaggerated, or maybe, and much more likely, it also included the number of bottles that the bartenders somehow managed to liberate for themselves.

There was much conversation around the bars. It never ceased to amaze me how loquacious some of us would get with a drink or two under our belts. Even Bob Howard, usually rather spare with words, could become downright chatty.

After telling one of the sergeant bar tenders that he should always remember that he was keeping his eye on him, he went on to say that as soon as it could be arranged, maybe they could begin to bring in a few comely Korean ladies to help with the bartending.

"Well, Sir," the bar sergeant responded, "that would be great. But where would we find them?"

Success to Stalemate in South Korea

Bob downed a bit of his bourban and water. "Maybe we could check out some of those South Korean Army women around here."

The sergeant laughed. "Aren't they supposed to be off limits to us GIs?"

"Details, Sergeant, just details. We'd only pick the good-looking ones."

"I don't know, Sir. I haven't seen any that look that good to me, not even just for screwing."

Bob laughed. "We had the same problem when I was in the Philippines. We'd only pick the ones that were lighter colored than a brown paper bag."

The high point of the evening was auctioning off the eagle rank insignia of the out-going regimental commander, of course a "bird" colonel. What with the general uproar, I didn't follow the proceedings very closely, since I was embroiled in conversations with Hal Evans, a new battalion surgeon, and Bob Riley, the chaplain, while discussing a trip we might take to Mexico when we got back to the States. It turned out that one of the battalions wound up with the eagles, for the top bid of $475.

Of course, by the time we had done a few chouses of "Behind Those Swinging Doors," we had forgotten all about the auction. It turned out that the officers of the battalion that won the eagle rank badge were quite surprised, since the officer doing the bidding for them was Macdonald of the Division ambulance outfit. I never did hear whether any money ever actually changed hands.

The next day brought more rain, and many of us who had participated in the revelry the previous evening were understandably rather subdued. That evening we had another Western for a movie, the rain obligingly having stopped at sundown.

As usual, Honsho and the rest of the South Korean houseboys that the outfits in the regiment had acquired were there. They still very much preferred being houseboys with the GIs, rather than taking their chances on being drafted into the ROK army. But what they had learned about life in the United States was, to a great extent, being drawn from watching those movies that we had nearly every evening when the situation permitted it.

As the result, most of them became convinced that America was mostly populated by gun-toting cowboys, rebellious and hostile Indians, gangsters and mean cops. We did our best, when we had the occasion, to try to dissuade them of these ideas, but the language barrier, despite our patois of Korean, Japanese, and English, seemed hardly up to the task.

On the 24th, three of us planned to take a trip over to the town of Yangyang on the eastern coast of South Korea, facing the Sea of Japan. It was probably not really a legal thing to do, although the lateral road was well behind the lines, because much of it ran through territory under the jurisdiction of ROK divisions.

First, there was sick call, and then there was the matter of the battalion commander who felt like he might be getting a cold. So, he decided to sweat it out by wrapping himself up in a blanket and lying out under the hot sun that, at least temporarily, had replaced the rain. When I saw him, he had been heavily sweating, but had nearly stopped doing so, was febrile, felt almost too weak to stand up, and had a dry cough. He had clearly become somewhat dehydrated, almost to the point where one could well worry about impending heat stroke. I got him into the shade of his tent, removed his blankets, and started an IV of half-normal saline solution as a way to quickly correct his fluid balance. Young and healthy, he soon came out of it, but I told him to drink water, and take it easy.

Just before noon I decided to make lunch out of canned soup, cheese, plus beer that I had been saving, for Armstrong and Riley who were going along on the trip. Afterwards, one of the guys from regimental S-3 came by and was passing out notes that stated that, "Peace proposals are not under any circumstances to be discussed with reporters." What peace proposals? We had heard nothing about any such thing.

The lateral dirt road running west from our positions near Inje to Yangyang, 40 miles away, was not too bad. The

Success to Stalemate in South Korea

three of us plus a jeep driver got away at 1300. Three ROK divisions, side by side, were positioned along the road. The traffic was much lighter, since the South Korean outfits didn't seem to have anywhere near as many vehicles as ours did.

Yangyang turned out to be a small town that was actually three kilometers inland from the water of the Sea of Japan. The white, sandy beach was rather pretty but quite empty. The wave action seemed to be far less than on the western side of the peninsula where the tidal changes could run as much as 15 feet or even more. This had presented great problems for the Marines and the army division accompanying them when they conducted their justly famous assault landing at Inchon under fire the previous September. We walked around for a while, enjoying the scenery, while the driver cleaned the jeep's spark plugs, and then we headed home.

Again, Bob Howard dropped by to ask me if I would consider putting off rotation, and stay with Collecting as he planned to do, since he had been promised a promotion to Major. He assured me that I also would make Major almost immediately, and it would then be only a very few more months until I would be rotated. I did think about it, but remained unconvinced.

At 2300, I went by to see the battalion commander. He was clearly doing a lot better. He insisted that I take two bottles of bourbon with me as I left.

On the 26th, we heard that a group of new medical officers had come to South Korea. Considering the number of medical officers still on TDY, I had to doubt that there would be enough of them for one to be my replacement.

It was also announced that henceforth, the time to be used for official reports would be Greenwich mean time, which, of course is British time since that is where Greenwich is, and is pretty much the standard all over the world.

The next day, we moved down to Hongchong, a hot, dusty trip of nearly 50 kilometers, or about 30 miles, from Inje. We were still on reserve status. Since there seemed to be some sort of problem with my W-2 form for 1950, I wanted to go down to Division Rear, now in Wonju, to see if Finance could straighten it all out.

On the 28th, Mike Armstrong, coming along for the ride, and I took Honsho along, to drop him off near Sillim-ni, where his family was now living, for a five day visit. The trip was only about 20 miles, over fairly good roads, but it was hot and dusty. South of Wonju, the roads worsened. When there had been a war going on in the area months previously, the engineers had labored mightily to keep them open, but the area now was a sort of backwater.

We finally found the farmhouse where Honshso's family was living, although it took a bit of driving around to do so, since not having been there before, he hadn't been too sure about exactly where it was located. We finally found it up on the side of a low hill, actually a good distance away from what was left of the village of Sillim-ni. We let him off near a path that wound up the hill towards the house. Considering all the stuff that he was carrying, mostly a lot of food supplies, he faced a rather difficult climb up to the house.

At Finance, in Division Rear, I learned that for some unknown reason they had failed to prepare a W-2 form for me. So, they would have to send a message to the Army Finance Center in St. Louis to get the necessary information, a process that would take at least two weeks. I reluctantly recognized that in all likelihood I would still be somewhere on the Korean peninsula and be able to pick up the paper work.

The first thing we did after we were back to our area was to hit the nearby shower where we ran into some medical officers from a nearby clearing station. They were not only complaining about the fact that their new chief mess cook wasn't ordering enough coffee from supply, but were also upset because they had gotten the word that it would not be until September at least before any of them would be rotated. Some of the clearing station medical officers had arrived in Korea with the earliest of the army divisions, but were not considered to be working in actual combat zones.

I realized that those of us in combat infantry battalions, regiments, and their supporting units were considered to be on a different schedule.

After dinner that evening, I had a couple of drinks at a going away-party for one of our MSC officers who was being rotated. The recent beginning of peace talks with the Chinese that we were now hearing more and more about was becoming a main topic for discussion. While we knew little about the substance of the talks, we were inclined to be rather skeptical about them, since we were all very much aware of the sporadic heavy fighting that was still going on.

George MacDonald showed up as the party progressed, having brought back a couple of crackerbox ambulances assigned to Collecting that had been serviced by the Division motor pool. While we were chatting, it occurred to me to ask him about how things were going with that battalion that had been having all of the integration problems.

"From what I hear," he said, "they're doing pretty damned well."

"That's a relief," I replied. "They must have finally sorted out a lot of problems."

He took a sip. "Good point. However, I did hear that they got pretty thoroughly investigated by a special delegation from the NAACP."

"I guess they must have passed inspection."

George nodded "I also heard that after they showed the delegation around, they invited the members, all dressed in army uniforms but without military insignia, into a tent, and brought out a couple of bottles. Everything was apparently very buddy-buddy."

I almost laughed. "I guess that means that they got along pretty well."

"Yeah, but there was something else. I also heard that as the meeting broke up, a black army officer with the guys in the delegation stood up, and said something to the effect that, 'You gentleman may think you've got the racial integration problem pretty well sorted out, and maybe you have here. However, just you wait until you get all these men back to the States where there are ladies around. It sure won't be the same.' "

This month of June was, we had heard, supposed to have been a very wet month, but it certainly hadn't been so far. The streams and rivers that had been over-flowing so recently because of the earlier rain storms were now very low. It seemed to be getting hotter and hotter as the sun blazed relentlessly down from the brassy sky.

As the month came to a close, because the hot weather made sanitation more difficult to enforce, I had to be ever more vigilant about inspecting the various regimental mess set-ups. During the inspection tour of one company mess I ran across a sergeant I had last seen during our retreat from Kunuri the previous November. He was still bitching about how we had been told by our high command that General MacArthur had proclaimed that the Chinese armies were just a bunch of laundrymen, and if they ever encountered the U.S. Army, they would promptly turn and run away.

Late in the afternoon, a flat bed truck with a load of ROK women soldiers, also rather rudely known as the "whore corps," stopped on the road that ran by the battalion area. There was instantly some suspicion that this was not entirely coincidental, since this day, the last of the month, was well known as often a pay day for the troops. The women put on a little song and dance show using the flat bed of the truck for a stage, and then announced that for $10 from each of the spectators, they would put on a longer show. They insisted that the money be in the new script that had just been issued. The longer show was more of the same and not at all salacious, perhaps much to the disappointment of the GI audience. The South Korean money, called the "won," was then down to something like 6000 to one against the U.S. dollar.

More information soon came through about a cease-fire arrangement being discussed at the Pan Mun Jom talks, although we really hadn't learned any more about the details. The rumor going around was that if such a deal really happened, our division might be sent to Europe. Of course, many months earlier, after we had pretty well chased the NKPA out of South Korea, and before we were sent up into North Korea on that ill-fated and disastrous campaign, the rumors were all about how we would all soon be sent to Indochina to help the French fight the communist Indochinese.

The next day, the First of July, the replacement for the long-gone Naval medical officer finally showed up, so I was able to return to my regular post at Collecting as soon as I had him properly oriented to his new job.

CHAPTER 40

A visiting colonel, who was Chief of the Assignment Section in the Army Surgeon General's Office, held a meeting at the nearby MASH the next day, the 2nd of July, for the medical officers in the area, to explain the newly instituted rotation program for medical officers. He also discussed the problems that had occurred while implementing it.

He told us that the Secretary of Defense, who had visited South Korea the previous April, had prepared a memorandum summarizing the need to set up programs for replacing not only the Navy medical officers that had been lent to the Army and the Regular Army medical officers on temporary duty, but also for rotating the other medical officers as well. It was duly forwarded to Eighth Army GHQ in Japan for transmission to the Army Surgeon General's office, the SGO, in Washington by radio. A receipt for the document was duly filed.

The SGO was well aware that other branches of the Army were well along in setting up rotation programs. However, domestic demands for dealing with the flood of casualties coming in to Stateside hospitals, and demands for the staffing of European military hospitals because of the "Cold War" build-up, seemed to have become predominant in medical officer assignments. For some reason, the Far East command seemed to continue to be getting a relative few from the replacement medical officer pool, despite the "Hot War" in South Korea. Of the 150 medical officers to

Success to Stalemate in South Korea

be coming out of the Medical Field Service School in June, only 30 were said to have been scheduled to be sent to South Korea.

It wasn't until the 2nd of June that the memorandum was finally discovered. The first page of the message, the cover sheet, was what had been received and filed, but the rest, for some reason, had become detached from it. This must have contributed significantly to what had seemed like delays in the formation and implementation of Army's plans for rotating medical officers.

After a national draft program had been put in place, reportedly out of 850 young doctors of draft age who had been offered commissions as medical officers in the Army, less than 50% immediately accepted them. Also, a new Surgeon General had been appointed as of July 1st.

We also learned that a group of medical officers, now being promised for the end of July, would be coming our way to take care of replacing the last of the temporary duty medical officers. It was unclear whether there would be any left over to replace those of us in the line outfits. Another group of 300 was scheduled to arrive in South Korea during September.

In the meantime, they were also considering rotating some of us to Army hospitals back in Japan. Since I had been told that I was now one of the five medical officers that had accrued the most combat time in the division, I was hopeful that I could somehow be replaced before that program could get fully underway. All in all, it was a most informative and illuminating session.

That evening, we had a send-off party for the White battalion commander. The other officers were all new. After the party, which didn't last too long, the lieutenant colonel that was taking over the command of the battalion decided to rout out the troops, sort of like the new broom that sweeps clean. He was, of course, concerned that civilians were selling the GIs bootleg whisky, because we had seen empty bottles of it scattered around. One was labeled "Old Scotch No. 1 Whiskey." We couldn't be sure that the "whiskey" didn't contain wood alcohol, which was very unpleasant stuff indeed. I also remembered how, a few months earlier, we had caught some of our GIs rolling cigarettes containing straw from the ubiquitous Korean mats made of hemp that was a close cousin to marijuana.

We found two GIs who were out like lights, and there were a couple of dozen more who were too drunk to be able to stand up. We sent the two unconscious ones off to the nearby Clearing Station. The problem we were just discovering was that the perimeter guards we posted at night seemed to be turning their backs when civilian whisky sellers came around. Maybe they were being bought off with free bottles.

There were also problems with what were called ROK "Special Services" outfits that were beginning to come and go in the area, mostly after dark. Many of their female members were apparently readily available for a suitable amount of current military script. A sergeant in a supply outfit based down in Wonju was caught bringing up a small group of Korean girls to provide similar services. A warrant officer reportedly took off his insignia of rank and stood in line one night to pull off a one-man raid, although it was not entirely clear as how extensive his investigations were.

CHAPTER 41

The next morning I took along the new battalion medical officer, who had finally arrived, together with two of our senior medics, while I made sanitary inspections of the various messes in the regiment. He soon showed me that he needed very little clueing in about how to properly perform such inspections. Since he seemed to have his other duties as a battalion medical officer already well in hand, I could now move back to Collecting.

In the course of our inspections, the mess sergeant of the regimental tank company mentioned that he had an oversupply of coffee and was almost desperate to get rid of it. So, as a plan began to form in my mind, I graciously offered to relieve him of the problem, which meant that we drove away with twenty ten pound cans of coffee beans. It was close to the truth that more military equipment including mess supplies seemed to change hands in the Army through a barter system than by being issued by the supply services.

I remembered hearing how some of the Clearing doctors were bitching about how their new mess sergeant still wasn't ordering enough coffee and they were always running out, since he had yet to understand how much coffee they really drank. This was of course partly because so many of their casualties came in late in the day and even during the night.

I then drove myself down to that clearing station with the cans of coffee secured in the jeep. My main purpose, ostensibly, for the trip was to check out how the two GIs that had passed out after drinking Korean moonshine were doing. However, I had other plans as I carefully parked the jeep near the clearing station mess tent.

After finding out that the two GIs had awakened in reasonably good order, but that they were planning to hold them for another night to make sure they were okay, I got into a conversation with one of the doctors. As always, the most common subject was rotation. He mentioned that he had heard that medical officer replacements were likely to be coming in faster than we had been led to believe, which was good news, if true.

On the way back to my jeep, I stopped by the hospital mess tent and engaged the young mess sergeant in conversation. It turned out, as I had suspected, that he was quite low on coffee. He said he had only joined the unit as a replacement two weeks previously, and admitted that when he ordered coffee for the mess for the first time, he had no idea of how much of it was consumed by their personnel.

I knew that the trip was worthwhile when he also mentioned having an excess of grapefruit juice, so it wasn't long until I struck a deal with him to trade two cases of it for the coffee I had brought along. I was pretty sure that, being a recent replacement, he might not be aware of the fact that grapefruit juice was rather highly prized for mixing with, and diluting, 190 proof medical alcohol for drinking purposes. I quite failed to mention that it was possible that the reason why he had so much grapefruit juice on hand was for that very reason. Of course, I also failed to mention that my plan was, by such bartering, to work up to acquiring one of the gasoline-powered refrigerator units that were now being issued, if I didn't get rotated first. No matter what, the grapefruit juice would be welcomed in Collecting, and certainly not go to waste.

A regimental officer's meeting was called that afternoon to sort out the details of our regimental combat team's review by the commanding general and a visiting Assistant

Success to Stalemate in South Korea

Secretary of Defense, planned for the next day, the 4th of July. Included would be not only the three battalions, but also semi-permanently attached units, such as artillery, tanks, and engineers. In sum, they formed a Combat Team. I elected myself to provide medical support for the event, which would mean that I would be able to stay in Collecting's reception tent. As hot as it usually was in the daytime, it was not unlikely that some GIs might pass out after standing in formation.

After a quick trip through the chow line for dinner, Major Henry Buckley, our new collecting station commander, and I drove over to the Division area. Along with 10,000 or so other GIs we stood waiting on dusty rice paddies and after half an hour, military vehicles brought in the touring Jack Benny show. Since it was only a small troupe, they could use a flat bed truck for a stage. The show was very well received. We appreciated seeing him so far from home.

Afterwards, we fought our way back through the mob to our jeep. Henry started to laugh when I raised the hood, quickly took the distributor rotor and the cable from the coil to the distributor out of a pocket, and replaced them. We always removed these vital parts when we parked a vehicle anywhere away from Collecting to make sure it would still be there when we got back. Henry sounded a lot like his predecessor, Bill Sloan, when he commented that it was all just something else he had to learn.

There was just enough time to return to Collecting in the gathering darkness, and be there for the start of the nightly movie. This time it was one entitled "The Fat Man," not a bad whodunit.

On the next day, the 4th of July, the big review went reasonably well. Since it had become overcast, it was also notably cooler, if still muggy, even though it hadn't rained for a while. There were, fortunately, no problems with GIs falling by the wayside during the review.

Conversations now more and more often revolved around the rumors of peace negotiations. Most of us continued to be skeptical about them, even though we realized that we still had only the scantiest of relevant information. We hypothesized that the communist enemy was cooperating with such talks only because it would permit them to surreptitiously go about reinforcing their forces and positions without having to worry about our aircraft harassing them, while they prepared for a massive assault that would again attempt to take over all of South Korea.

We also thought that with so many communist infiltrators from the north already seeming to be south of the 38th Parallel, the North Korean and Chinese armies would have no problem at all taking over South Korea if our troops and those of the other participating countries from the United Nations were to leave the peninsula any time soon.

The rains returned again the next day. We also learned that we would soon be again going north to replace a Marine regiment. Then, in a couple of days we had another regimental inspection. It was blistering hot this time, but the inspection did not take long. Only four GIs had to be disciplined. The inspecting general said that our regiment was the best he had seen but we wondered if he was in the habit of saying the same thing to all the outfits that he inspected.

CHAPTER 42

While I was glad to be back in the regimental collecting station, I had to admit that the battalion headquarters where I had been filling in had a better mess. Perhaps it was because our original cooks had all been rotated, although their replacements, just like the replacement medics, all seemed to be pretty well trained. Almost all of the original Collecting Station MSC officers were already gone, except Bob Howard. Some of them had been replaced by senior sergeants who had been given field commissions. Henry Buckley was already doing his best to wangle a transfer to a MASH unit since he was also a qualified surgeon.

It all reminded me that I should be making some after-the-Army plans myself. I had decided that I wanted to get into a residency program in Internal Medicine after being discharged from the army, which most likely would be in June of 1952, and at a university hospital hopefully somewhere in California.

On July 12th, I received a memorandum from the Eighth Army Surgeon's office, in Taegu, assuring me that I would be rotated in August. It was at least some consolation. We heard that afternoon that our regiment would be moving out in four days to take up positions in the Hwachon reservoir area near Yanggu where we would replace a Marine regiment, confirming what we had been told previously. The Marines would in turn move back into our present bivouac area as soon as we vacated it. We were also to carry with us the sports equipment that we had been using while in reserve in case things became even more static than they already had become. We thought that this was because of the peace negotiations that were continuing in Kaesong.

Persistent low-lying fog caused several dreary days. It was almost as if it wanted to rain, but couldn't quite. Units of the Marine regiment that we would be replacing on the line began to pull back and move in around us.

Since we were seeing no casualties beyond routine sick call, well before noon one day I was able to take a litter jeep and drive over to the battalion aid station now commanded by the medical officer who had been transferred there from the Division Forward aid station. The aid station wasn't busy, so we had the chance to sit around, and spend time just conversing, or as they would describe it in those days, "bull shitting," or even less elegantly, "fucking the dog." We had a great old time of it reminiscing about when we were interns at hospitals in the States. We also discussed the curious plight of a fellow in a surgical residency at a large university hospital. He had refused to accept a commission as an Army medical officer, and was now facing being drafted into the army as a private.

We were just getting up to eat lunch at the mess of one of the battalion's line companies, when Bob Riley showed up, again demonstrating that the chaplains were unparalleled in sensing where and when someone had opened a bottle. We had to first have a couple of drinks with him.

On the way back to Collecting, I stopped to say hello to the guys in a Marine regimental collecting station that had just moved in. While they had excellent medical equipment, they had set up only two pyramidal tents and a couple of squad tents. In contrast, our collecting station was operating out of our new sectional hospital tent, six squad tents, two CP tents, one pyramidal tent, one small-wall and one large-wall tent.

We were all out of the sack by 0330 on July 17th, and, once packed up and loaded, traveled by convoy up to our new positions. We arrived there just as the day started to warm up and finally banish the fog. Our bivouac area was in a rather narrow valley near a little town named Yachon-ni. It was east of Yanggu and south of the eastern tip of the Hwachon Reservoir. We set up our tents on a wide sandy area bordered by trees and the road. A shallow and rather picturesque little creek wound it's way under a rather rickety bridge and down between our bivouac area and the road. We could cross the creek to the road on broad stepping stones, and it was easily fordable by our vehicles without using the bridge. All in all, our set-up seemed as good as any we had had, and the roads to our battalion aid stations were reasonably passable.

The only patient I saw that day was an air tac officer with an infected sebaceous cyst on his head. Air tac officers were usually Air Force pilots on temporary ground duty who were attached to infantry outfits to control air drops of supplies, strafing runs, and bringing in helicopters for casualty evacuation.

Later, it became rather cool. After it got dark there was a bright moon illuminating drifting cumulus clouds surrounded by brilliant stars. Then, the clouds coalesced and it started to rain again. A tent was found where the motion picture projector could be set up, and we watched a fairly decent movie.

There was no question that the war really did seem to be winding down. News that the peace negotiations now involved arguments over the issue of how to evacuate the foreign troops from the South Korean peninsula spread quickly through the ranks. I was cheered on the 18th to learn that the Deputy Surgeon of Eighth Army had visited Division Forward and had announced that replacement medical officers were definitely on the way. He also was reported to have said that the "Old Guard" medical officers, and I was sure that included me, would probably all be rotated out within the next thirty days.

CHAPTER 43

The intermittent heavy rain continued. Our routine remained rather boring. No combat casualties were coming in. All there was to challenge our medical capabilities was sick call, and there wasn't much of that, either. Possibly self-inflicted wounds were mercifully only a memory. Our main activity, other than training new replacements, seemed to be little more than continually checking to see that our tents were properly ditched to keep rainwater from running through them. It was fortunate that we continued to get a lot of reading material. And, there continued to be a movie nearly every night.

By the 21st of July, the rains began to slacken. It again turned very hot and humid. We finally had some action when a patrol from one of our battalions tangled with a booby trap, leaving several wounded, two of them rather severely. Later, in anticipation of being rotated soon, I packed up my winter clothing along with a pair of Korean slipper-like shoes I'd picked up, stuffed the lot in a barracks bag, and mailed it off to my home address. My day was made on the 25th when a GI came in with what I was sure was a clear-cut case of polyarthritic rheumatic fever, as it was called then.

Otherwise, the monotony was soon broken when two regiments in another division were ordered to take two adjacent hills that were north of their positions. The higher one towered to almost 1200 meters. The North Koreans were

Success to Stalemate in South Korea

using it as another very effective observation post for aiming their artillery, of which they seemed to have been getting a lot more just recently. Indeed, it was estimated that they could observe our troop activities for nearly 200 kilometers to the south, a very definite advantage for them.

Those hills would undoubtedly be heavily defended. The enormous military advantage to be achieved by gaining control of them was quite obvious. The planned assault was somehow claimed to be well within the newly-imposed limitations on combat activity in order to avoid casualties as much as possible.

We could hear, and see, the intense artillery bombardment of the hill that began that night. It was foggy, precluding much air observation and support. We heard that the battalion making the initial assault on the taller of the two hills met little resistance early on. Then the NKPA, firing from deep and well-prepared trenches nearer the top of the hill, really opened up. Nonetheless, the GIs managed to make some headway, if rather slowly, even though the enemy seemed determined to keep the hill under their control.

Towards evening, we heard that an artillery shell had fallen short and pretty well erased one of the line rifle companies assaulting the hill. Another company was hit by napalm from a misguided American air strike with even more disastrous results.

That night, we could hear the intensive artillery fire that was targeting the NKPA positions. Fog rolled in again in the morning, and then suddenly, the sun broke through. This helped the forward observers to better aim their artillery as well as permitting air tac officers to call in air strikes. We then heard that by evening, lead elements had finally almost reached the top of the hill, where they dug in for the night.

It was no secret that a quickly-emerging problem was that the GIs in the ranks had no intention of risking becoming the "last casualty" of the war, and were thus singularly disinterested in exposing themselves unduly to enemy fire. It was rumored that in one line company, sixteen GIs flatly refused to go on the attack. It was even also rumored that they were executed on the spot, although it seemed hard to believe, as were most such rumors that were always flying around through the ranks. There was no question, though, that the peace talks did not much favor any heroics amongst the soldiers on the front line.

The hills were finally taken, although there were still scattered pockets of stubborn enemy that had to be eliminated. There had been a lot of casualties on both sides, although our regiment's outfits had not been very heavily involved. While ultimately successful, the enormity of the battle hardly seemed consistent with the widely-heralded objective of limiting operations to avoid casualties.

We heard that the visiting Eighth Army Surgeon had confirmed that we five medical officers who had been in Korea since the previous July would be rotated by the middle of August. It was also said that we might be flown back to the States, which would take two days, rather than returning the more common way by troop ship that would take about two weeks.

By the 28th, there were still a few pockets of North Koreans almost fanatically defending their positions. Nonetheless, we were not receiving many casualties from our battalion that was now participating in the attack. I did sew up a gash on the head of a counter intelligence agent who had sustained it while swimming in the nearby river.

When we learned that the two hills had at last been completely cleared of enemy, we hoped that the whole operation would at least strengthen the hand of the American admiral in charge of the peace negotiations for the United Nations.

We also learned that Eighth Army was not at all happy with the way that many of our troops had behaved during the recent action. The air support was also judged to have had serious inadequacies. There had been, apparently, more problems than just that misdirected napalm drop and the "short" artillery shell that we knew about. Of course, as noted, a large part of the problem was very likely due to

Success to Stalemate in South Korea

continuing widespread and undeniable reluctance amongst the GIs to become the "last casualty."

The month of July, and the anniversary of my arrival in Korea, ended with stifling hot and humid weather, punctuated by periods of drizzling rain. In many ways it reminded me of summers in the Midwest, even to the massive numbers of mosquitoes. Mercifully, we continued to have a near-endless supply of DDT insect repellent, and continued to use it generously.

We were enjoying a remarkable plentitude of beer, as well as the whisky rations, as we waited with increasing anxiety for the peace negotiations to come to some sort of desirable conclusion. The military actions we were undertaking were now little more than patrol activities, which involved only occasional skirmishes with similar small groups of the enemy. We wondered if they, too, were beginning to wind down their activities while awaiting the resolution of the peace negotiations.

There were now no new plans that we knew of for large scale military operations anything like what we had been involved with during the previous winter and spring. However, while the official word from Eighth Army still emphasized that all operations should continue to be planned and executed to minimize casualties as much as possible, the GIs no longer gave it much credence.

CHAPTER 44

The hot and humid weather, not surprisingly, continued into August. The collecting station remained in the same place, with no evidence of any plans to move, as we had so often done in the past to keep up with our line battalions. They hadn't been moving much since those hills and the adjacent territory had been secured.

Replacements continued to come in as our personnel were rotated out, so it was necessary to keep our indoctrination classes running. Still, I found that I often had time to read a book a day. More and more reading material had become available. We continued to have motion pictures nearly every night as soon as it got dark, still most often "B" pictures but nonetheless welcomed. Our new mess cooks were doing much better, undoubtedly because they were getting not only better rations but also more experience.

There was only limited patrol activity. Now that we possessed those two hills, our line outfits had excellent defensive positions. However, the GIs in those line outfits didn't seem to have much faith in the ongoing cease-fire talks. We were given very little information about their progress, or lack of it.

On the 2nd of August, all the nearby shower units were out of operation for one reason or another, so some of us bathed in the clear water of the creek that ran past our bivouac area. During the evening we got in some casualties from one of the battalion's patrols that, in the dark, had inadvertently wandered into an enemy minefield. One of the men had a badly shattered leg, probably the one who had stepped on the mine. Since he had been treated in the battalion aid station, all we could do was to adjust the splint on his leg and the tourniquet, and send him off as quickly as possible to the nearby Clearing station. I was thankful that the road back was a relatively good one, and the ambulances could make good time even at night.

Torrential monsoon rains suddenly began on the night of the 4th of August. Our previously docile little creek soon became a wide, raging torrent. The little bridge was soon washed away, and I realized that the branch APO, the army post office up the creek a mile or so, also had problems when I saw the mail order window float by. We had to move some of our tents to higher ground, a complicated matter in the dark. The engineers put in a temporary footbridge the next day, but we had to carry patients back and forth across the swollen river from the collecting station to the MSR by using amphibious trucks borrowed from the Engineer battalion. The rain did seem to keep down the mosquitoes.

The next day, the engineers also provided us with a rather large section of a Bailey pontoon bridge. However, since the rain had stopped as suddenly as it began, the water in the creek soon receded and there wasn't enough of it left to float the pontoons. We weren't seeing too many casualties, but the ones we were seeing were often badly injured since most were the result of unlucky encounters with booby traps and land mines, with some due to sporadic enemy mortar fire. Patrols were ranging ever further out amongst the hills north of us, which were rugged enough in many areas to make casualty evacuation difficult. At night, it often poured rain, of course warmish. It was often very foggy in the early morning, and later in the days there was oppressive heat and humidity. It somehow seemed to me that the weather was worse than it had been at the same time the previous year.

We were very much cheered, even jubilant, at the news from X Corps that 50 Medical Corps officers would be due to arrive in a week, with another batch coming in the next month. I immediately wrote my wife about making tentative plans to meet up in San Francisco, the most likely place where I would enter the States. On the 9th of August, we learned that what we hoped would be our replacements were due into our area on the 15th. I placed a call from our field telephone to the main Army PX in Japan to order a 12 place set of Noritake china and a camphor chest to be sent home as presents.

The rains became more insistent. Indeed, it had rained every day of the month so far. By now we thought that we were well aware of where the water in the little creek would tend to flow when it tried to become a river, and had rearranged our tents accordingly. Even so, on the night of the 11th, it poured harder than ever before, and our little creek again became even more of a fast-flowing river. We soon had to hurriedly move several tents again.

Barefoot with our trousers rolled up to the knees, the ambulance platoon leader, Macdonald, and our new dentist who had replaced Ramirez joined me in rescuing our beer supply from it's now-endangered "ice box" hole near the stream. It was a job we didn't want to leave to the enlisted men, of course. Since it was such a warm rain, we didn't worry much about getting wet.

The engineers' pontoon bridge section was soon washed out. The major was marooned back at Division. Communications with our battalions and their aid stations were knocked out, although we could raise Division Rear by radio, about 40 kilometers down the road behind us. One of our battalion's headquarters was washed out, and another regiment's headquarters was completely marooned on what became a sandbar.

CHAPTER 45

On the 12th of August, the next day, I was notified that my name had come up on the R & R list again, which seemed to be rather ironic. I felt surer than ever that I had done the right thing by turning down the offers of promotion to Major, if I would stay with Collecting for a few more months, when I learned that the replacement medical officers had already come up as far as Taegu.

Our routine now varied very little from day to day. At around 0630, Honsho, now back at Collecting, would stick his head into our tent, and say, "Major, Captain, chop-chop now!"

We would then fight our way out of our sleeping bags, now the lighter summer-type ones. We slept in our shorts and white T shirts, and draped our green cotton twill shirt-jackets and field trousers across the framework supporting the mosquito nets over our cots. If you inadvertently got your elbow up against the net while asleep, that elbow would be a swollen mass when you awakened because the mosquitoes would bite right through the net.

I also draped my pistol belt over the framework with its holster for my .45 caliber automatic pistol on the right side and my canteen on the other. The shoulder holster that I had worn for so long had become useless months previously when one of the straps broke.

The morning of the 13th was gray and fairly warm. We walked the short distance over to the mess tent at

0700, and sat down at a fair sized table that could seat eight. We got there just as several other officers were getting up from the table.

Breakfast was ham and eggs with hot biscuits. Pak, the mess unit's South Korean houseboy, as usual presided over the serving. He had the names of common dishes all written out so he could remember them. We would tell him how much to serve by saying "toksan," Japanese for a lot, or "scoshi," for a little. Just for the hell of it, we would also order such things as, "A half a toksan," or perhaps, "two scoshis."

On this day the coffee was good, and we lingered a bit. We would usually rehash whatever it had been that we had been discussing the previous night. This time it was the movie we had seen, which had been unusually good with lots of double entendres. By 0800, we were ready to face the day. The war didn't seem close at all.

In the meantime, Honsho had set up two pans with warm water and two canteen cups with cold water. The one was for shaving, and the other was for brushing our teeth. The tent sides had already been rolled up, for better ventilation, and our sleeping bags had also been rolled up and placed at the heads of our cots. That morning I had to call Division on the field phone, and then the adjutant to get official clearance for rotation. I received it, but was also told that I couldn't be released until the 21st of the month.

Sgt. Henderson came by with five field medical tags from patients evacuated from the Battalion Aid Stations. Even if a soldier could be housed in our holding tent for one or two days, treated, and then returned to duty without being evacuated, a field medical tag would be completed and forwarded to Division's personnel section to be included in his personal records.

Three of the five complained of prolapsed hemorrhoids, another complained of eye trouble, and the fifth complained of high blood pressure. By the time I got to the reception tent, another patient was added who was quite jaundiced and clearly had what was then called infectious hepatitis.

The three with hemorrhoidal complaints proved to have just that. The eye problem turned out to a pterygium, a fleshy growth on the eye that was irritated. We had been seeing quite a few cases of hepatitis. It was a bit mysterious, since while we knew that hepatitis was caused by a virus, exactly how it was transmitted was not then well understood.

Experience in and after World War II had shown that the blood plasma that was used as a temporary blood volume expander could cause hepatitis because the blood from some of donors from which it was made unknowingly carried the viruses and there was then no test for such. It was also discovered that if plasma was left on the shelf for six months or so, such viruses would become inactivated.

Earlier in the war we had blamed hepatitis on the GIs getting into native water wells that were contaminated, but that didn't seem to still be a problem. Some thought it to be the result of too much drinking over time, but the GI's were too young to support that idea. It was finally realized years later that it was our methods of giving inoculations for disease prevention that was the major factor in transmitting the hepatitis virus.

A soldier with high blood pressure, and assigned to a Battalion Motor Pool, presented a more difficult problem. He said he didn't feel sick. I asked how he knew he had high blood pressure, a very unusual finding in a 20 year-old. He replied that one day he felt a little dizzy, and had gone on sick call at the Battalion Aid Station. As the medical officer examined him, he checked his blood pressure and found it to be high. He said that the dizziness soon subsided and then he felt fine. However, the medical officer had him come back several times to recheck his pressure, and said it was always elevated.

High blood pressure, so seldom seen in the age group of our soldiers, could suggest serious problems. The Battalion Surgeon confirmed that he had been checking the young man's blood pressure repeatedly and it was always up. I didn't have enough room on the tag for all the information, so I wrote everything out on another tag to also go with the patient.

All six were put into an ambulance and sent back to Clearing. It was notable that with the war going the way it was, we were seeing far fewer suspected malingerers, or "gold bricks."

I then retired to my tent, prepared to read another mystery story. As soon as I opened the paperback pocket book, there was Sgt. Henderson again, this time with two more FMTs in his hand. He had been a medic in the infantry in Europe, and after the war joined the National Guard and also qualified as a registered nurse. Because so many of our original medics had been rotated and replaced, he was now the best qualified to be our First Sergeant. His overly obsequious manner was almost too much at times. However, appreciative of his abilities, I just signed the tags. Both were relatively minor injuries but clearly needed to be evacuated.

I took off my shirt/jacket, since it was getting much warmer, and let my dog tags hang down outside my white tee shirt. A phone call came in from Division that confirmed my release for rotation. I had no sooner hung up the field telephone when another call came in from a Battalion Surgeon.

He needed a helicopter to evacuate two GIs in one of his Battalion's Line Companies that were dug in up on a hill. The GT's had been playing around with a hand grenade that unexpectedly exploded, wounding them both severely. It had taken the medics almost two hours to carry them down the tortuous paths from their foxholes on a rugged hilltop to a place on the valley floor that was suitable for a chopper landing and take-off site.

I immediately called the Division Surgeon's office and gave the map coordinates of the nearest landing place, and described the area and how badly wounded the two men were. The call would be relayed to the nearest MASH, and they would send a chopper from their attached helicopter group, which usually numbered three or four of the Bell H-13s. I then called the Battalion Surgeon to tell him that a helicopter would be on it's way, and told him to get his medics and the patient out to the landing site so they could signal to the helicopter where to land, since it didn't have a radio. While this all seemed a bit complicated, it was far less so than earlier in the war. I had to keep in mind that since using helicopters for medical evacuation was still relatively new, it had taken awhile to get proper procedures for using them sorted out.

Back in the Collecting reception tent, I looked over the operational reports the clerk had prepared covering the past 24 hours. They always had to be carefully gone over to check for grammatical and spelling errors, too often to the extent that they had to be laboriously typed all over again. When they were all in order, I signed them, and had a few words with two of the newer replacements about learning our procedures. And then, it was nearly time for lunch.

Feeling thirsty, I went around to the new "ice box" hole where we kept the beer. The hole had been dug amidst some bushes near the creek, the coolest place available. I pulled back the wet GI blanket covering it, and downed one of the cans. Lunch was soup and hot dogs, not one of the cooks' better culinary efforts. An MSC officer from one of the Battalion Aid Stations, one of the few old hands left, was visiting us. We drank coffee and talked rotation until 1300.

Returning to my cot, I was halfway through the paperback book, when the field phone rang again. The call was from another Battalion Medical Officer who had been with us for only a couple of weeks. He reported that he was sending in four GIs who had been wounded when one of them accidentally stepped on a land mine while on a patrol, that they were getting the men ready for transfer, and also mentioned that their beer supply was running very low. I didn't ask him which issue he thought to be the most urgent, but I did promised to investigate. Then, I phoned the medical officer with the Division Forward Aid Station to see if he had heard anything new about rotation. He told me that he hadn't heard anything.

I settled down to read again, and had just rearranged the mosquito netting when Sgt. Henderson, as it started to rain again, came in through the tent flaps, carrying four

EMTs for the land mine casualties. I followed him back to the Receiving Tent.

The one who had stepped on the mine, a sergeant who had been leading the patrol, had a rather badly injured lower leg. Luckily for the other three, they were only lightly wounded. They had all been treated at the Battalion Aid Station, so that all our medics had to do was check the dressings.

After we checked the Field Medical tags, the men were cleared for evacuation on to Clearing. The man with the injured leg had to be transferred on a litter, but the other three were able to sit up. The crackerbox ambulances would speed them back to the Division Clearing Station, the distance now being only a half mile.

Within a few minutes the field phone rang. It was a call from the Medical Officer out with Division Artillery. He was also sweating out rotation, and was checking in to see if I had heard anything new, which, unfortunately, I had not.

The rain became heavier, doing little to reduce the heat, much less the humidity, and the creek rapidly filled again. I decided to write a letter or two. Then, Sgt. Henderson was back, saying that another casualty from the patrol was on a litter jeep on the other side of the creek that was rapidly becoming a river again, and that the amphibious truck we had been using to cross it until the bridge could be rebuilt was off somewhere else. He also said there was a nearby place where the water was shallower.

The two of us waded out to the litter jeep. The driver had fashioned a poncho over the wounded man to protect him from the rain. I made sure that bleeding was under control, the tourniquet was correctly applied, and that the IV drip of plasma was infusing properly. The sergeant checked the Field Medical tag to make sure that penicillin has been administered in the Battalion Aid Station. We also made sure that also that the wounded man had been given enough morphine to control pain. The sergeant didn't have to be told to get a crackerbox ambulance to ford the stream, help the driver transfer the wounded man on a litter into it, and send the caualties on to the Division Clearing Station

With my pipe lit, I decided to drop by the eight-man tent where the other officers bunked. Since it was now quiet, most of them, including a visiting line company Captain, were sitting on cots, idly smoking while they waited for the rain to cease.

Soon, the drizzle stopped. I stuck my head out of the tent entrance and yelled at Honsho to drop the sides on the smaller tent that the Major and I used in case it started to rain again, since the mosquito netting replacing the rolled-up sides of it didn't do much to keep out rain water. Indeed, it soon started to pour for perhaps ten minutes, stopping as abruptly as it started. Weather could change very quickly.

The sky was clearing, promising a real sunset, as we sat down for dinner. As we ate, we talked, mainly about the medic whose brother had been killed three months or so previously. We had noted that he seemed to be going a little sour, and it didn't seem as if it was just over the loss of his brother. In any event, he would soon be due for rotation.

Sgt. Henderson came by, saying softly, "Sir, I think I have a case of Hansen's Disease in a Korean. It seems to have taken most of his nose."

I could not brag about having seen many cases of Hansen's Disease, the newer and preferred name for what they used to call leprosy. The man was a middle-aged South Korean farmer who had been drafted to be a carrier for an ROK army unit but had deserted to go back to his farm. He apparently had stopped at one of our Battalion Aid Stations on his way home to see if they could do anything for his nose, most of which was missing. The Aid Station, understandably, sent him on to us in Collecting.

We now had an IPW unit at Regimental Headquarters. IPW stood for "Interrogation of Prisoners of War." They sent over one of their people, a Sergeant. He spoke fluent Japanese. At that time, of course, almost all South Koreans also spoke Japanese, at least to some extent, after being forced to learn it during the previous four decades of

Japanese occupation. I would talk to the sergeant in English, and then he would talk to the patient in Japanese.

Other than missing so much of his nose, the Korean didn't have any of the other skin changes usually seen with Hansen's. I wondered if the problem was possible late syphilis, or even skin cancer, since as a farmer he would probably have often had his nose exposed to the sun over the years.

After about a quarter of an hour of rather difficult and ponderous interrogation, we decided to send the man back to Clearing to see what they could do for him. I asked the Sergeant to ask him where he was originally from. Before the sergeant could translate my words into Japanese, the man turned his head to look at me and said, "Wonju."

CHAPTER 46

On the morning of the 14th of August, I drove a jeep with a trailer down to the Division Surgeon's office to pick up two new medical officers, one to be my replacement in the Collecting Station, and the other to relieve a Battalion Surgeon. Needless to say, I drove them back most carefully. Official orders had finally come through for me to be rotated in three days, which would be on the 17th.

I dropped my replacement off at Collecting on the way back, and after introducing him to the other Officers and the non-coms, I took the other Medical Officer out to his Battalion Aid Station. The Medical Officer being replaced promptly produced a bottle of Scotch to celebrate the occasion. Naturally, I had to stay for a bit just to be sociable.

When I got back to Collecting, it was immediately apparent that in the meantime the Major and the MSC Officers had been doing their best to clue in my replacement and I wondered if they were scaring the bejesus out of him in the process. He proved to be most thoughtful in that as I arrived, he smiled, and reached down into his barracks bag, still at his feet, and fished out two bottles of bourbon and announced that he wanted to share them with us. Of course, we very graciously accepted his offer.

It was soon apparent that, as it had been the case with the other medical officers recently sent to us, his four months of training in Field Medicine before being sent to

South Korea was far beyond the little preparation that I, and most of my contemporaries, had

received. The recent turnabout in the way the war was being waged would probably mean that things would be far less exciting for him than what I had experienced during the war's earlier days. As far as the new men coming in as replacements were concerned, the hectic

events of those first six months of the war, July through December 1950, were little more than ancient history.

Our Division had now advanced to near the Kansas Line. However, there were problems with the enemy digging in on the increasingly rugged and hilly terrain north of us. The area was known by the heights in meters above sea level of the three prominent hills.

The fact that the enemy now seemed to have a lot more artillery available than ever before was disquieting. It was also apparent that that Eighth Army was hell-bent on capturing those hills to protect our positions, again with little apparent concern about minimizing casualties. An ROK Division that presumably was especially well trained was to make the initial attack on the 18th, with backup from the American forces. We were told that there was the chance that, sooner or later, our Division might also become involved. I realized that I would be long gone before that would happen.

By mid-morning on the 16th, I had finished packing and getting my gear squared away for my departure the following day, including giving my burp gun away because I realized that I had no chance at all of getting it through Customs when I returned to the States.

I took the time to visit our three battalion aid stations that were set up amongst the foothills north of us and bid them farewell. I also had saved three bottles of whisky for presents. I borrowed a jeep, and set off up the MSR. The three Aid Stations were fanned out about two miles from each other, two on the line and the third a bit behind the other two since their Battalion was in reserve.

I was already quite familiar with the way to get to the first one. It was set up rather comfortably in a little valley with hills on three sides. The Aid Station shared the area with an Artillery Battery of 105mm howitzers. As I arrived, the new medical officer was being oriented by the medical officer he was replacing. I recognized none of the personnel assigned to the Aid Station, the others having long since been rotated. We could hear the none-too-distant artillery as the assault on those three hills was beginning. When the Medical Officer being replaced wondered why he was not going out on the same day that I was, but rather on the next day, I really had no answer.

After an hour or so, I left, drove back through the Artillery outfit's positions, and found a dirt road, little more than a path, that the map I was carrying assured me led to the other Line Battalion's Headquarters area. It turned out to be more complicated than the map suggested, but I finally found the Aid Station. It was set up by the side of the so-called road in a grove of spindly trees that gave good cover, if they ever needed it, for their vehicles. It was lunchtime so I ate with them, remembering that their battalion headquarters had a good mess. Again, there were few men there that I still recognized.

Realizing finally that if I was to have time to go by the Third Battalion Aid Station, I had better get moving. I said my good-bys and left another bottle behind. I had to drive back down the narrow dirt road to the MSR. While this Battalion was in reserve, it was not positioned very far behind the other two. As I came to another dirt road that I hoped was the correct one to take me to it, I noticed that a hundred meters or so along the way there was another Artillery Battery set up near the edge of a little valley.

When I got closer, I could see that the howitzers were remarkably well protected by having been dug in and there had been an extensive use of piled-up sandbags to surround them. This was a little unusual, but since the start of the peace negotiations, many line outfits seemed to be consolidating their positions with sandbags and digging in ever deeper, perhaps because they now had more time to do so. Beyond the Artillery positions, the road became little more than a path, dropped down to cross the little valley and then ran up and over another low hill.

I stopped by the Artillery unit to make sure that I was going in the right direction. I was told that I was, but to be careful, because the North Koreans dug in to the north had some mortars registered on the dirt road where it crossed the valley. They then warned me that every once in awhile they would try to drop rounds near vehicles using the road, but they hadn't been doing so for several hours. They thought that the enemy probably didn't want to fire off too many rounds at any one time for fear that our artillery forward observers would figure out exactly where the mortars were located and turn the big guns loose on them. I nodded, and said I'd be careful.

As I put the jeep in gear, the little valley ahead looked almost unbelievably peaceful. Mindful of what I had just learned I decided not to dally. In the rear view mirror, I could see that I was raising quite a dust cloud behind me, but at the time thought little of it. Going up over the hill on the far side, I soon came to the Battalion Headquarters tents, and beyond them the Aid Station.

Of course, I broke out the remaining bottle. I knew this Battalion better that the others because of the times I had gone out there to fill in at their Aid Station. The new medical officer seemed to have really gotten the hang of things. His equally new MSC assistant was eager to talk about how things had been in the past, and how they were beginning to dig in, just like that Artillery Battery.

When it got to be 1600, I realized that despite enjoying the conversation as much as I was, it was time to leave. After I stood up, if a bit unsteadily, I thought to ask about the road back where it coursed through the valley. They all laughed and said that, yes, the North Koreans were shelling it every once in awhile when it was daylight, but as far as they knew they hadn't hit anything yet. That seemed reassuring.

I started up the jeep, and headed back down the road, soon reaching the point where it dropped down into the valley. I was about halfway to the far side when I heard an unmistakable karumph. In the rearview mirror. I could see smoke and debris kicked up not more than 100 meters behind me. I slammed the throttle to the floor, and started to zig-zag the jeep as much as I could without going entirely off the narrow dirt road. It seemed like an eternity until I finally crested the hill.

As I passed the Artillery outfit, the first thing that I noticed was that the artillerymen standing around, and who had obviously been watching the whole thing, were laughing their heads off. With considerable constraint, I just waved as I sped past them. There would be a party in Collecting that night for those of us being rotated.

CHAPTER 47

On the morning of the 17th of August, those of us being rotated were taken with our stuffed barracks bags in 6x6 trucks down to Hoensong, now the site of an ever-expanding Army base, where we spent the night on folding cots in a Quonset hut.

We were then taken down to Wonju the next day where we were given boxes of C-rations and loaded on a train waiting at the railhead. The ancient coaches had no seats but instead had been rigged with three shelf-like wooden structures along both sides, one above the other, for carrying wounded on litters. The shelves were too close together for sitting up, so we had no choice but to simply lounge back on barracks bags. The glass in the windows, if there ever was any, was long gone. It didn't matter much, since we wanted as much ventilation as possible to help mitigate the humid heat.

The train was pulled by an ancient coal-burning Japanese locomotive. The lack of windows made the overnight trip to the south rather filthy, particularly when going through the all of the railroad tunnels in the South Korean mountain ranges. However, we didn't mind it much at all because we were finally on the way back to the States.

We arrived in Pusan about noon on the 20th of August, and were quartered overnight in a converted school building close to the harbor. I found it rather interesting that the depot for incoming replacements was located some distance away on the other side of town. The next afternoon we boarded the rather rickety-looking Koan Maru, one of the Japanese ferries that made regular trips back and forth across the Sea of Japan from Sasebo on the southern-most of the Japanese home islands to Pusan. While still at the dock we were serenaded by an Army Band playing all sorts of popular tunes of the day and doing it very well indeed.

Our ferry was the first to leave Pusan for several days because of rough seas due to the mid-August monsoons. The sky was clear but the sea was still quite turbulent when we departed, but after several hours it became calmer. There was a sort of mess arrangement on the ferry, involving large pots over fires and an awful smell of fish. I was glad I had the C-rations.

We were supposed to get further orders while at an army base in Sasebo. If none came through within 7 days, we would be shipped up Camp Drake up near Tokyo, where I realized I could connect up with the luggage I had left in Japan.

Only about half of the officers being transferred back to the States were actually getting definitive orders in Sasebo within that time frame. Most of them were being taken by train up to Camp Drake near Tokyo to ship out by Merchant Marine ships that took 10 to 12 days at sea to reach a U. S. West Coast port. Only a lucky few shipped out on trans-Pacific airplanes, since the seats on them were usually reserved for men on emergency leave, couriers, personnel on Special Orders, and ranking officers. One way or another, it was estimated that most of our group would be on the way home by no later than the 30th of August.

There was a large officer's mess at the base in Sasebo where we were quartered while we rather anxiously waited. Men from all of the US armed forces mingled in the bar with those from the other countries of the United Nations who had troops in Korea. We were no longer wearing field uniforms, but rather khaki long-sleeved shirts with khaki ties and trousers.

John Benton

One night a few of us got to talking with some Australian artillery types in the busy bar. One of the Aussies suddenly frowned, turned to me, and said, "You know, sometimes you Yanks can give me a bloody pain in the arse. You all seem so damned proud of being descended from the English!"

CHAPTER 48

No orders had yet come through for me when, on the 28th of August, I was told that I had been selected, along with four other officers, to take a group of enlisted men by train up to Camp Drake, near Tokyo, for transfer by air back to the US, as we would be.

I was stunned when I found out who the four other officers were. I would have believed that they all would be infantry types. However, there was a chaplain, a line company Captain from the Battalion I had first been with early in the war, another Medical Officer who was a friend of mine, and an officer from the Division's Judge Advocate General's office.

It wasn't until the next day that I found out how this curious mix of officers had come about. It seems that one of the clerks in the Sasebo base office had been a litter bearer assigned to my Battalion Aid Station earlier in the war. Although my memory was hazy about it, it seems that I had promoted the GI to Corporal, not long before he was wounded and evacuated on the eve of the disastrous battles near Kunu-ri in North Korea.

When he recovered, he was sent back to duty from a hospital to a clerk in the offices of the Sasebo base. He apparently was given a list of the names of all the officers waiting to return to the US and told to pick five at random, when he recognized my name. Then, he picked out the Captain of the Infantry Company to which he had earlier been assigned. When he had found out that his wife was divorcing him, he felt grateful to the chaplain who had helped sort things out, and to the Judge Adjutant General officer who had helped him. For the fifth one, he picked a Medical Officer that he somehow knew was a friend of mine.

The train trip up though the very scenic rural Japanese countryside, on the afternoon of August 30th, was relatively uneventful. We had three coaches on the end of the train for the personnel we were escorting, who were all very happy at the idea of being on the way back to the States. There was a small section in one coach for we officers. It might be noted that a bottle or too had been brought along to ease the rigors of traveling. The rest of the train was packed with Japanese civilians.

Running right on schedule, the train was almost quaint, quite old-fashioned, and very clean. One interesting feature was that the "benjos," the toilets at the end of each coach, were simply a closet with a hole in the floor. The idea was to squat over the hole and do your business. Toilets, particularly in rural areas, were often much the same except that many had catch tanks for what was to be used as fertilizer.

We were met at the station by Army buses, and were taken to Camp Drake, a large Army base near Tokyo. After hurriedly getting settled into my assigned quarters, I headed for the bar at the Officer's Club.

The first guy I ran into was my surgeon friend who had been sent to Korea in the early days of the war and had been subsequently reassigned to the big army hospital back in Tokyo. He was standing all by himself at the bar and rather gloomily smoking a cigarette. I hadn't seen him since the previous April when I was on R & R, and had since often wondered if he had ever sorted out his rather complicated domestic situation.

I tapped him on the shoulder to get his attention, and said, "Well, for Christ's sake!"

He turned, his eyes lighting up, and replied, "You old son of a bitch. What the fuck are you doing here?"

Success to Stalemate in South Korea

"Just trying to get the hell out of Asia in general and Korea in particular. Are you waiting to ship out?"

"Yeah, I guess so," he said, as he lit another cigarette off the one he had been smoking. "That's what they tell me."

I waved to get the Japanese bartender's attention. "At least you sure lucked out by getting rotated out of South Korea last February."

"Better believe it. Anything's better than being stuck in that God-forsaken country."

"You were lucky as hell to get out of this stupid war so soon after it started."

"Christ," he answered, "I sure know that."

Getting out my pipe and tobacco pouch, I asked, "How long have you been hanging around here?"

"A couple of weeks." He downed his drink in a gulp.

"I thought we're supposed to ship out by boat or even airplane real soon after we get here."

He took a long sip from his glass, and said slowly, "I guess I missed a couple of flights."

The bar was beginning to fill up and get noisy. As I picked up my scotch and water, I said, "Did you ever sell your car?"

After a moment, he nodded. "Yeah, finally, to a Marine colonel stationed in Tokyo. Didn't get a lot for it. But, as long as this war is going on, there's no way I could have it shipped back to the States."

I lit my pipe as I realized that he probably wasn't about to discuss his musame. "Is there any way we can get out of here and see a little of the town?"

He shook his head. "Well, if there aren't any flights that will be available for awhile, you can, but they don't want you to get too far away in case there's an unexpected flight."

As I was finishing of my second Scotch, it occurred to me that he had mentioned missing two flights. That certainly seemed peculiar. I couldn't imagine anyone in his right mind not wanting to get as far away from Korea as soon as possible. It was also apparent that he had been in the bar for quite a while before I arrived.

"You said you've already missed two flights. Isn't that kind of strange?"

He turned around and leaned back against the bar, a drink in one hand and a cigarette in the other. "I can talk to you, maybe the only one I can. I don't want to go back to the fucking States, strange as it may seem."

Incredulously, I asked, "You mean you would rather stay here?"

"It's not so simple." He waved at the bar tender. "I think you already know at least part of the story."

I nodded. He had, of course, told me all about it when I was in Tokyo on R&R the previous April.

"No, I really don't want to go back. I've been trying to get my orders canceled so I can stay here."

"You're Regular Army, aren't you?" I said. "All this can't be doing your career any good."

He said nothing for a moment, as he slowly shook his head. "I know. I've been doing my damnedest to get them to see things my way. The bastards have even restricted me to this area, so I can't even go off the base like you guys can. Maybe they think I might be an AWOL risk."

"If you're in the Regular Army, don't you have to expect being transferred around a lot?"

"Yeah, I know all that. It's just that I don't want to get sent back to the States right now."

Not knowing a whole lot about the intricacies of having a career as a Regular Army Officer, I didn't know what to say. It was quite apparent that what he really didn't want to do was to go back to his wife. Even though I realized that I needed another drink like a hole in my head, I signaled to the bartender.

"Couldn't they court-martial you for refusing to obey transfer orders?"

"I suppose so," he said slowly. "I still keep thinking that maybe I can still persuade the bastards."

I shook my head. "That sure isn't the way things work as I understand them."

He picked up a new drink. After a moment he said, "Don't sweat it, buddy. It's not your problem."

He was right. Perhaps I was out of order. A couple of other medical officers joined us. My friend had little to add to the conversation.

CHAPTER 49

The situation at Camp Drake became just another hurry-up-and-wait proposition. I saw my friend nearly every day. He remained morose, but we talked a lot, mostly at the bar in the Officers' Club.

Of course, I remembered that I had been notified that my luggage had wound up being stored at Camp Drake. Much to my surprise, I was able to easily retrieve it, in a Valpak mostly containing uniforms that I had to drop off before I left Japan for South Korea over a year previously. The multiplicity of tags on it testified to how much it had traveled around. I took out the uniforms, and while waiting for orders, had time to get them cleaned and pressed locally, and then put them back in the Valpak. I called the Japan Central Post Exchange to inquire about the china and the camphor chest I had ordered from South Korea, to learn that both had been shipped out on the 17th of August.

I finally received word that I would be shipping out by air on the 5th of September around midnight. On the 2nd, a group of us got permission to go off the base to a very fancy nearby Japanese restaurant to celebrate.

That night, in the Officer's Club Bar, our group was gathered. There was some discussion about where we should go to celebrate. I was talking to an officer who had been a chaplain in one of our division's regiments.

Success to Stalemate in South Korea

Just then, another officer stood up, and blew three blasts on his whistle. A few other officers stood up and started towards the door.

I knew that there would be just about all the pedicabs in the area lined up at the door.

The chaplain said, "Where are all those guys going?"
"Off to a fancy restaurant somewhere," I replied.

"Maybe we should follow them."

I didn't have a better idea.

So, our little group went out to the line of pedicabs, and two to a cab, we followed the others. It was a short run in the humid twilight to a nearby building that was quietly elegant and inconspicuously located well back from the busy street in a grove of well-trimmed trees.

After we climbed out of the pedicabs, we lined up as we entered the ornate front door. An older woman in a kimono, standing behind the door, greeted us by bowing to each of us as we bowed to here. She was undoubtedly the mama-san of the establishment.

Then, after removing our boots and leaving them to one side of the entryway, we all rather solemnly proceeded in our stocking feet down a short corridor, made colorful by expensive-looking drapes on the walls.

We then entered a rather long room that was decorated after Japanese fashion, and took our places on mats placed along a long, low table. It was set with bottles of saki, wine, as well as Scotch and Bourbon. Each place was also set with ivory chopsticks and shiny brass goblets.

Soon, Japanese ladies dressed in elegant kimonos silently took their places just back from the table. When an officer pointed his finger at a bottle, they would pick it up and refill his goblet. They, they served the many courses of an elegant Japanese dinner. It was surprising how behaved the young officers were, after their often-raucous behavior in the bar in the Officers' Club. It was as if they were duly impressed by the solemnity and grace of the servers.

After the slow-paced dinner, which, due to the inevitable toasting, took all of two hours, we all stood up, and following others that seemed rather familiar with the establishment, soon found ourselves in a room that was like the shower room in a high school gym.

There was a side room with places to put our clothes after we took them off. After taking showers, ladies in plainer kimonos silently handed us large towels to wrap around our now-naked bodies, as well as sandals that we called "flip-flops." We then proceeded outdoors in the humid warmth of the summer evening to rows of large hot tubs along both sides of a path, each under a thatched conical roof. Lights were strung in the over-hanging branches of trees.

We were assigned two to a tub. After tossing the towels to one side and gingerly lowering ourselves down into the very warm water, we could sit on a bench that ran around the inside of the tubs about a foot below the surface of the water.

Soon, girls in kimono-like robes, seemingly somewhat younger than the women who had served us dinner, appeared. I had learned that these were the "B" girls. The women who had served us during dinner were the "A" girls and were ordinarily not involved with the hot tubs, although I supposed that they might have been available for such if the price was right. The younger girls apparently understood little English, but were well trained to give massages. However, it was generally understood that they were also quite willing and capable of providing more services than just that.

One to each tub, the girls removed their robes and, giggling, jumped into the tubs stark naked. I was beginning to wonder how my friend the chaplain would react all this, although he did have plenty of wine during dinner.

The festivities were restricted by the fact that the pedicabs didn't run after midnight. After we got out of the tubs, dried ourselves off with the towels, retrieved our uniforms, and made it to the front door to get our boots, we had to deal with the mama-san, now seated at a portable desk near the door. We soon discovered that what we had to pay, above and beyond the price of the sumptuous dinner, depended upon on what had gone on in the hot tubs. The charges seemed to be divided up in to categories of "no play-play,'" "scoshi (a little) play-play," and "toksan (a lot of) play-play." As far as I could tell, the lowest price actually being charged was "scoshi play-play." I got stuck with it, even though I should have had the right to protest. My friend, the chaplain, however, got hit for "toksan play-play," and was clearly quite embarrassed.

There were some who preferred to spend the night. I was told that along another pathway there was a row of little hut–like structures with beds. A "B" girl was assigned to each of them. The game started with a man also in each hut. After a while, someone would blow a whistle, and the men would all change huts. This, apparently, could go on all night, and was known as "Blow the whistle changee-changee." I have no idea how much the mama-san charged for all that, but it couldn't have been exactly cheap.

The next day, the 3rd, two days before we were to be shipped out, I was awakened with a severe, and most urgent, case of gastroenteritis. I not only felt like hell, I didn't dare get very far from a latrine. Of course, I suspected that the tasty food at that Japanese restaurant was the cause of my visceral woes.

I visited the camp dispensary and scrounged up several codeine tablets that I hoped would at least partially calm down my symptoms, some benzedrine tablets to offset the sedative effects of the codeine, and sulfathalidine tablets to take just in case my problems were caused by a bacterial infection. I realized that such afflictions usually lasted for only a couple of days or so, and fervently hoped the medications would somehow get my insides under control soon enough so that I could get on the plane.

With the medication, I managed to get through that day without too much trouble. However, later that afternoon, the Colonel who commanded the base had me paged to report to his office. He told that he wanted me to take the responsibility of getting my friend on the plane with me. Just as I had feared, the colonel confirmed that since he had already missed two flights back to the States that he had been ordered to take, my friend was indeed in danger of being submitted to punitive action if he missed another. His requests to stay in Japan had all been rejected, because he was being assigned to a large Army hospital in Texas. All I could say to the Colonel was that I would do my best, and to myself I hoped that in the meantime I could keep my gut under control. He gruffly commented that what he was telling me I should consider to be an order, not just a request. I also wondered how in hell the colonel had found out that the guy was a friend of mine, and what might happen to me if I failed to get my friend on the airplane.

I tried to eat lightly, and was able to get through the night without too much trouble. However, when the codeine's effect began to wear off the next morning, the symptoms began to return. I tried more codeine. It soon seemed to control my extremely restive gut. However, I was afraid that I might have to take enough of it to almost knock me out, despite my obligations.

As I thought about how go about getting my friend on the plane, I realized that it would probably have to involve getting him drunk. I rather gloomily realized it would mean that such an approach would mean that I would have to be doing a lot of drinking myself, which was not at all appealing, given the unstable state of my insides. I surely didn't want to have anything to screw up my getting on that plane, after having looked forward to it for so long.

I paid another visit to the dispensary, and convinced the personnel there to let me have a lot of codeine tablets, as well as several more benzedrine tablets. All of this did finally succeed in keeping my gut quiet. Indeed, I was beginning to feel a lot better. Maybe the combination of codeine and benzedrine was working well, maybe it was the sulfa drug, or perhaps the disease had run it's course. I took it easy all afternoon, packed up my gear for the trip home, and sent off a telegram to my wife about meeting her in San Francisco in a couple of days and asking her again to make a reservation at that hotel where we had stayed before. I didn't leave my room in the BOQ until dinnertime. By then, I was, mercifully, feeling relatively normal.

Success to Stalemate in South Korea

In the officers' club, the bar was busy by 1800. Several officers there that were to be on the midnight flight were already getting a bit hilarious. I ordered a Scotch, and put a lot of water in it just to be safe. Almost too mindful of what the colonel had told me the previous day, I then searched for my reluctant friend.

At first I couldn't find him. I chatted with a few of the other men who would be on the flight, and they hadn't seen him either. With another Scotch in hand, with a lot less water, I even checked out the mess area where a few officers were already eating dinner, but there was no sign of him.

Then, it occurred to me to see if he might be outside, and I went to the front door to investigate. There he was, walking towards the door, with a taxi driving away behind him. I knew he wasn't supposed to leave the base, and for a moment wondered exactly what in the hell had been going on, although I easily guessed the answer.

After quickly walking back to the bar, I turned around, as if I had been there all the time, as he opened the door. He looked like he was on the way to his own hanging, which, from his point of view, may have been just what he was thinking. I hailed him, and walked over to join him for the last few steps back to the bar.

I waved at the bartender and ordered him a drink. He stood there for a moment, lit a cigarette, picked up the drink, and drank it down in one gulp.

Then, he slowly said, while again waving at the bartender, "The bastards are really on my ass."

I nodded, started loading my pipe, and decided I wouldn't ask him where he had been since it looked a lot like he'd been able to somehow sneak off the base, undoubtedly to spend some time with his musame. I certainly didn't want to mention what the Colonel had told me, and my orders about getting him on the flight back to the states.

Somewhat lamely, I commented, "Well, at least getting out of here by air should be one hell of a lot better than two weeks on a goddamned troop ship."

"Samo-samo, either way," he grunted. "All I can do about it is to get bombed."

I tried not to exhale too noisy a sigh of relief. My job may have just become a lot easier. I said, "Let's get a couple of drinks, and go harass those guys down at the end of the bar who'll be going with us."

He turned to look down the bar. "Those bastards are so happy it almost makes me puke."

Two drinks later, he had started to smile, at least rather wanly.

When it was time to board the buses, no pain was being felt by any of us. We were taken out to the Haneda air base where we boarded a C-54, actually a civilian airliner converted to military use with a civilian crew. After we dropped off our bags to be loaded, I had to help him up the portable stairway to the cabin of the four-engined transport aircraft. The accommodations were uncomfortable canvas seats, much like benches, along the sides of the plane's cabin. The space for feet in the center aisle was diminished by mysterious crates of things like Japanese china that had somehow been spirited aboard.

We sat in order by rank, the highest near the rear cabin door. Few sober breaths were being drawn. My friend fell sound asleep soon after we got on the plane. When we took off just after midnight, he appeared to be quite oblivious to the fact that we were, at last, airborne and on the way home. I was almost overjoyed when I realized that my insides were remaining settled down, perhaps thanks to all the codeine, since the restroom facilities on the plane were quite primitive.

CHAPTER 50

The C-54's cruising speed over the Pacific Ocean was said to be about 170 mph. While the seating arrangements were anything but comfortable, what the hell, we were going home. We stopped rather briefly for refueling at Wake Island, just as we had on my first flight to Japan so many months previously, but this time they had a new crew to take us the rest of the way

The next stop at Rodgers Air Force Base in Honolulu was where we had to go through reentry US customs and immigration procedures. Our belongings, much to our surprise, were very carefully searched for any drugs that we might have been trying to smuggle into the States. I was reassured in that I had been absolutely right in that I would never have gotten away with trying to smuggle in that Russian PPSh "burp gun." Later, we had a little time to do some shopping in the airport's shops and pick up newspapers and magazines.

On a glorious September evening, we flew over the Golden Gate Bridge nearly 48 hours after leaving Japan. The C-54 touched down at the Fairfield-Suisun USAF base near Sacramento, from where I had been flown to Japan 14 months previously. I had dozed off, but awakened as we turned on final approach for landing. My erstwhile friend, who was sitting on the other side of the plane, was awake, and rather glumly staring at his unfolded wallet, very probably at a little picture of his musame. He said nothing at all to me.

In the rush to get through the checking out procedures and collect my Valpac suitcase after we disembarked from the plane, I lost track of him. I never heard from him again, or anything about him, much less learned how things had worked out for him. However, I had done my job as ordered, if I really wasn't too happy about it.

Once out on the street curb with our gear, four of us hurriedly teamed up to hire a taxi, costing us $25 each,

for the 55 mile trip to downtown San Francisco. I was dropped off at the hotel where my wife had made reservations. It was very good to be back in the States.

The End

ABOUT THE AUTHOR

After I was discharged from the US Army in June, 1952, at the time being a medical officer at Camp Cook Army Hospital, in California (now the site of Vandenberg Air Force Base), I pursued a residency in Internal Medicine in Los Angeles at a university hospital. I had an active private practice in Los Angeles while living in my native Pasadena, California, and was quite involved in medical organizations until my retirement in 1994. I have since remained active in other organizations. These have included Scottish-oriented groups, vintage auto clubs with some racing of vintage cars both here and in England, flying, and medical history. My wife is continues to be active in managing pure-bred dog shows. I have two adult children, a boy and a girl.

Made in the USA
Las Vegas, NV
15 March 2022